JEAN-PIERRE HEIM

ARCHITECT

JEAN-PIERRE HEIM

ARCHITECT

Copyright © 2003 by Jean-Pierre Heim

All rights reserved. No part of this book may be reproduced in any form or by any electronic or mechanical means, including information storage and retrieval systems, without permission in writing from the publisher.

Visual Reference Publications, Inc.
302 Fifth Avenue
New York, NY 10001

Distributors to the trade in the United States and Canada
Watson-Guptill
770 Broadway
New York, NY 10003

Distributors outside the United States and Canada
HarperCollins International
10 E. 53rd Street
New York, NY 10022

Library of Congress Cataloging in Publication Data:
Jean-Pierre Heim, Architect

Printed in China
ISBN 1-58471-041-1

Book Design: Kevin Stone

Contents

INTRODUCTION 7

HOSPITALITY HOTELS AND RESTAURANTS

Thalassa - *New York* 8
Capitol Music Theater - *Offenbach Frankfurt* 20
Bulova - *New York* 26
Club Med - *Dakar* 34
Luxor Palace - *Dresden* 46
Luxor Cinema - *Paris* 56
Cinepanorama - *Greece* 58
Chameleon - *Frankfurt* 62
Peace Gardens - *Lebanon* 66
Yasmina Hotel - *Morocco* 70
Hotel le Pavillon Bastille - *Paris* 72
Abajour - *New York* 80
Ichthys - *Paris* 84

STORES COMMERCIAL AND RETAIL

Puiforcat - *Paris* 86
Christian Lacroix - *Paris* 92
Revillon - *New York* 96
Baccarat - *New York* 100
Nicolas Feuillatte - *Paris* 102
Lancel - *Aix en Provence* 106

PUBLIC BUILDINGS AND OFFICES

World Trade Center - Ground Zero - *New York* 112
Assomption Church - *Paris* 116
Paris City Hall XVIII Arrondissement - *Paris* 120
French Trade Office - *New York* 122
Die Leiter - *Frankfurt* 124
Citaix - *Lyon/Nangis* 126

FURNITURE DESIGN AND TROMPE L'OEIL

Trompe L'oeil 130
Luxor Line - Egyptian collection 136
Furniture line 140

RESIDENTIAL

Apartment - *Paris I* 144
Apartment - *Paris II* 146
Apartment - Alwyn Court - *New York* 150
Trump Residence - *New York* 152
The Arlington - *New York* 154
Mykonos House - *Greece* 156
Essex House - *New York* 170

CREDITS 174

"Ce livre est un itinéraire, je l'ai fait avec ma famille, mes amis, mes dessins, mon appareil de photo.

Cet itinéraire, je l'ai crée au fil du hasard, de mes rencontres et des pays que j'ai traversé.

L'antiquité, l'archéologie, l'architecture, le cinéma, l'Egypte, la Grèce, et l'Italie, sont les acteurs de ma liberté créative d'image."

This book is a journey, which I took with my family, my friends, my drawings and my camera.

Serendipitously, the countries I visited and the people I met, became part of this journey.

Introducing Jean-Pierre Heim, Architect

Sophisticated people who find themselves impressed by a new retail store, hotel, restaurant, public building, commercial office or private residence know that their reaction is seldom accidental. One reason why these often highly visible examples of architecture and interior design have become such effective environments for their owners and occupants is the increasing participation of gifted designers like Jean-Pierre Heim in developing them. Jean-Pierre Heim is a highly regarded visionary designer who maintains a thriving interior design practice in New York and an equally vibrant international architectural practice in Paris and Athens. Mr. Heim has a degree in architecture from the École des Beaux Arts in Paris and attended the University of Illinois for specialized architectural studies. In addition, he was awarded the Delano-Aldrich Fellowship from the American Institute of Architects.

Founded in 1980, Jean-Pierre Heim and Associates Inc. (**www.heimdesign.com**) has developed a rich portfolio of private residences, office interiors, retail stores, restaurants, hotels and showrooms. The firm's clientele includes a wide range of organizations, embracing international businesses as well as private individuals. Puiforcat, Van Cleef & Arpels, Revillon, Baccarat, Christian Lacroix, Lanvin, Lancel, and Club Med are just some of its many notable clients.

However, Mr. Heim's interests go well beyond designing buildings and interior spaces. His in-depth knowledge of international markets enables him to act as an image advisor and liaison for U.S. and European businesses seeking to operate on both sides of the Atlantic. He is also a foreign French Trade Advisor of France.

As a world traveler with a special interest in the vernacular architecture of Africa, the Middle East, Asia and the Mediterranean, Mr. Heim enjoys immersing himself in the local culture and tradition for each of his projects. Whether he is working in New York, Paris or Athens, he takes a multi-dimensional approach to design. Paying extraordinary attention to detail, Mr. Heim will create a comprehensive design package for his client which includes client image, architectural concept, interior design, furnishings and accessories.

The spirit of design by Jean-Pierre Heim is captured in his unique treatment of each project, setting it within an appropriate cultural context and staffing the best local design and technical talent to ensure optimal results. Mr. Heim is multi-lingual, able to work closely with a wide range of international clients who speak English, French, Spanish, Italian and Greek. He has an excellent reputation for developing strong client alliances and achieving complete client satisfaction from concept through move-in, offering a full range of architectural and interior design services that include strategic vision, corporate identity, programming, design, production of construction drawings and construction.

It's easy to see why Mr. Heim's work is published in noteworthy books, newspapers and magazines around the world. In the pages that follow, the reader will see abundant evidence of Mr. Heim's creative gifts as a designer with a good eye for form, color, materials and context. Most recently, Mr. Heim received national television coverage in France on TF1 and CNN for his World Trade Center reconstruction proposal. Now it is the reader's privilege to explore the vision of Jean-Pierre Heim.

Jean-Pierre Heim, architecte

Pour toute personne à la sensibilité un peu aiguisée, être impressionné par l'aménagement d'un nouveau magasin, un hôtel, un restaurant, un équipement public, un immeuble de bureau ou une résidence privée, est rarement le fait du hasard. Que de tels exemples d'architecture et d'aménagement intérieur parlent ainsi de façon aussi forte à leurs propriétaires ou à leurs occupants tient à ce que des créateurs talentueux comme Jean-Pierre Heim se sont impliqués dans leur conception. Jean-Pierre Heim est un de ces designers visionnaires reconnus, capable de conduire tout à la fois une activité d'architecte d'intérieur à New York et une carrière d'architecte international à Paris et Athènes. Diplômé de l'Ecole des Beaux-Arts de Paris, il a poursuivi ses études d'architecture à l'Université de l'Illinois. Il a reçu le Prix de la fondation Delano-Aldrich de l'American Institute of Architect.

L'agence Jean-Pierre Heim & Associés, crée en 1980 (**www.heimdesign.com**), compte à son actif un ensemble très riche de résidences privées, d'aménagement de bureaux, de magasins, de show-rooms, de restaurants et d'hôtels. Sa clientèle inclut aussi bien des entreprises internationales que des commanditaires privés. Parmi eux, on citera Puiforcat, Van Cleef & Arpels, Revillon, Baccarat, Christian Lacroix, Lanvin, Lancel et le Club Med.

Cependant, les centres d'intérêt de Jean-Pierre Heim vont bien au-delà de l'architecture et de l'aménagement intérieur. Sa profonde connaissance des marchés américain et européen, lui permet de conduire une activité de consultant d'image au fait du business international de chaque côté de l'Atlantique. Jean-Pierre Heim est un Conseiller du Commerce Extérieur de la France.

De ses voyages à travers le monde, il a rapporté le goût pour l' architecture vernaculaire d'Afrique, du Moyen Orient, de l'Asie et des pays du pourtour de la méditerranée. Jean-Pierre Heim s'immerge dans la culture locale et dans ses traditions pour mener chacun de ses projets. Il travaille à New York, à Paris et à Athènes, mais développe une approche du design à plusieurs dimensions. Il porte au détail une attention très particulière tout en proposant à ses clients un concept qui décline l'image institutionnelle, l'architecture, l'aménagement intérieur, les mobiliers et les éléments d'accompagnement.

L'esprit et la signature du design de Jean-Pierre Heim tiennent au fait que chaque projet est un cas particulier conduit en relation avec un contexte culturel et une tradition locale, en s'appuyant sur un professionnalisme et un savoir-faire technique propres à optimiser les résultats. Jean-Pierre Heim parle l'anglais, le français, l'espagnol, l'italien et le grec il peut ainsi traiter et travailler étroitement avec une clientèle internationale. Sa réputation a pour base une solide capacité à nouer des liens étroits avec ses clients et à répondre à leurs attentes en développant des projets complets incluant aussi bien une vision stratégique, une identité d'entreprise, un cahier des charges, un concept de design, que l'ensemble des outils nécessaires à la conduite du projet et à sa production (dessins, construction).

On comprend ainsi que son travail fasse l'objet de nombreuses publications dans les journaux, les magazines et l'édition. Dans les pages qui suivent, le lecteur pourra se rendre compte en quoi consiste le talent de Jean-Pierre Heim: son oeil et son approche de la forme, de la couleur, des matériaux et du contexte dans lequel il travaille. Très récemment, Jean-Pierre Heim a été interviewé par TF1 et son projet diffusé sur CNN au sujet de sa conception de la reconstruction du Word Trade Center pour lequel il a proposé un projet. Il est temps maintenant pour le lecteur d'explorer la vision de Jean-Pierre Heim.

Thalassa

Tribeca, New York, New York USA

New Yorkers can now take an imaginary luxury cruise through the Greek Islands while dining on superb Greek cuisine at Thalassa (Greek for "sea"), a new, 4,000-square-foot, two-story restaurant, designed in 2002 by Jean-Pierre Heim and Sol Niego as architect of record, in fashionable Tribeca. Starting with the name given by the restaurateur and his Greek food importing family, doing business as Fantis Foods, Heim has drawn on his own memories of luxury vessels that sailed the Mediterranean in the 1930s to transform an historic building that once warehoused Greek olives and cheeses into a shipshape interior. Customers "board" Thalassa through the dining room on the upper level,

Upper: Staircase to lower level.
Lower: Atrium as seen from upper level.
Opposite: Fantail-like upper level balcony.

Left: A view of Tribeca from the upper level

which is fitted with a chestnut plank floor, walls of sheer, white curtains layered over the warehouse's brick, and a long, curving, backlit mosaic bar accented by billowing white sails and blue lighting overhead. Once inside, they can take a grand wood staircase to the lower level, where a 25-foot-high atrium evokes a ship's fantail and

Above: Rendering of upper level bar.
Opposite: Twin columns frame lower level onyx bar

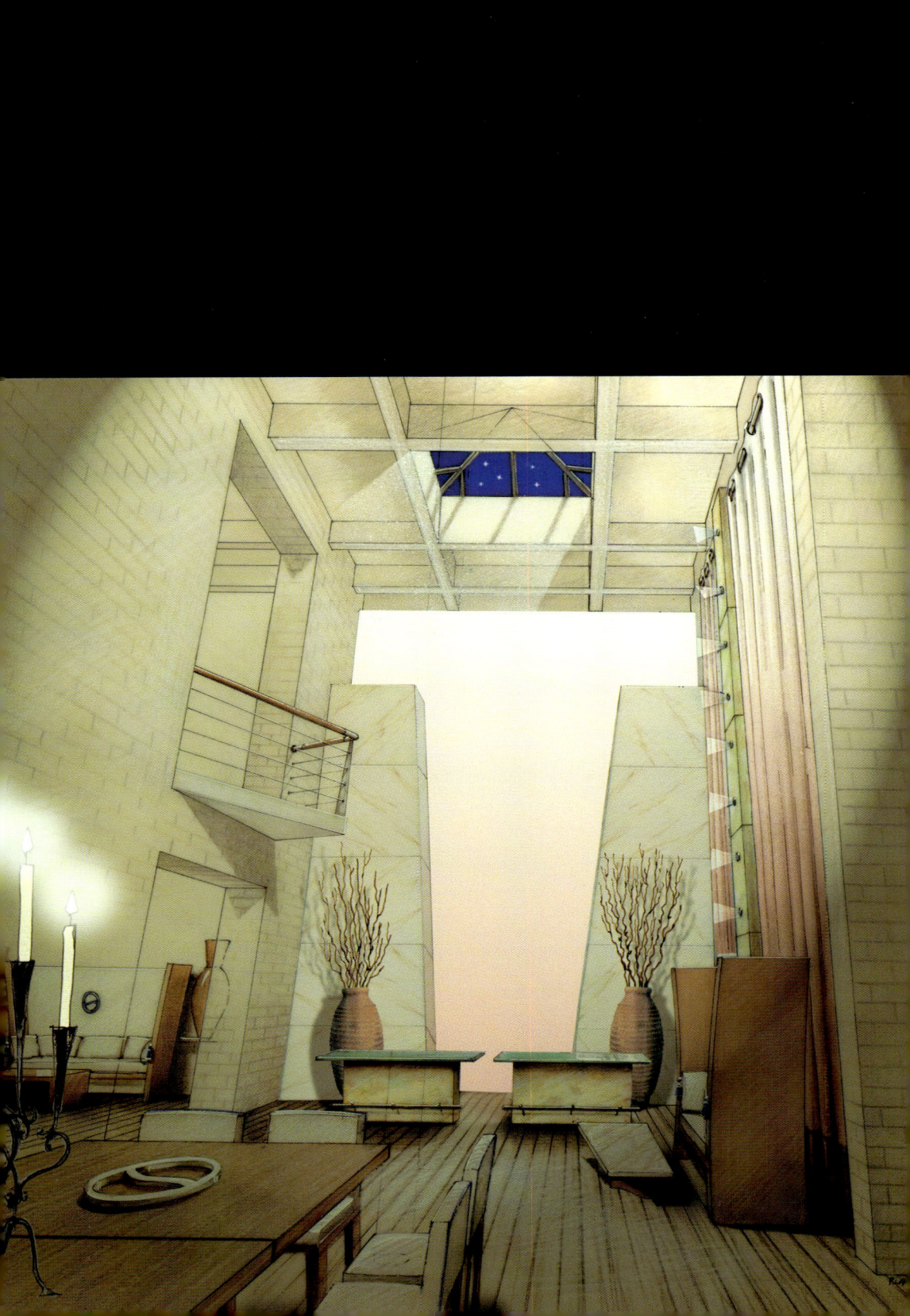

provides room for additional seating, a monumental, transparent onyx bar with two glowing, Mycenaean-style 20-foot-high columns, and a 40-foot-long wine cellar and cheese shop. Not only have magazine editors in the United States, France and Greece, and numerous restaurant reviewers lauded the design — the James Beard Foundation nominated it for Best Restaurant Design — New York radio station WCBS welcomed Thalassa to the existing restaurants in the neighborhood by proclaiming, "Hey, Nobu, there's a new guy on the block!"

Above: Onyx bar on lower level.
Right: Screen beside maitreBelow: Rendering of upper level bar.
Opposite: Twin columns frame lower level onyx bar.

Top: Detail of staircase joining upper and lower levels.
Above: Display in lower level wine and cheese shop.
Opposite: Casework showcase for wine selections.

Capitol Music Theater

Offenbach, Frankfurt, Germany

While Offenbach, a small German city on the outskirts of Frankfurt am Main, sees itself primarily as a business center, it now boasts an innovative cultural facility in an old historic building that should entice residents and visitors alike: the Capitol Music Theater. This multi-functional musical theater, designed by Jean-Pierre Heim in 1999 using Andrea Palladio's Teatro Olimpico in Vicenza, Italy as inspiration, has a raked, 650-seat auditorium as its centerpiece. However, in keeping with the needs of contemporary performing arts centers, the space can convert to an event theater that readily accommodates diverse activities like a concert hall or a discotheque. One of the earliest steps in the project's development was the creation of a brand identity. After the name Capitol was chosen, Jean-Pierre Heim designed the semi-abstract figure of a muse as the theater's symbol and had an 18-foot high sculpture fabricated in plaster and gold leaf in a Paris studio to serve as the model for statues of varying uses that are installed

throughout the theater. As for the basic spatial arrangement and architectural scheme, Heim has created a processional sequence that introduces guests to an atrium that retains its historic form, and subsequently directs them to orchestra seating on the ground level or mezzanine seating on the second floor, via a grand staircase, inside a

contemporary auditorium with a proscenium stage. The interior design is unequivocally meant to contribute to the audience's total experience. The atrium, for example, is cast as a severely elegant basilica with a colonnade of Doric columns in precast concrete, a floor of gray and black marble, and walls painted in terracotta

Upper left: Sculpture in lounge.
Upper right: Rendering of atrium elevation.
Opposite: Atrium with sculpture flanked by cypresses.

Below: Section displays atrium, auditorium and stage.
Opposite: Orchestra with standard seating and cabaret seating.

and inscribed with an Italian text, all under a barrel-vaulted skylight. Theatergoers confront the 18-foot high sculpture in the foreground, flanked by two cypress trees, upon entering. If they wish to enjoy food and beverage before the start of their program, they may choose between a lounge with a 70-foot-long bar on one side of the atrium, or a restaurant/bar on the opposite side. None of this quite prepares them for the theater's auditorium, however. This voluminous space, beneath a hemispherical dome, paints its walls, ceiling and mezzanine balcony in an electric blue that is dramatically interrupted by a 12-foot-wide section, a trompe l'oeil "slice of cake" that reveals a 17th-century, Italian-style theatrical interior, and contrasted with a marble floor in black and beige checkerboard bearing the theater's logo. If this isn't excitement enough, there's always the show to follow.

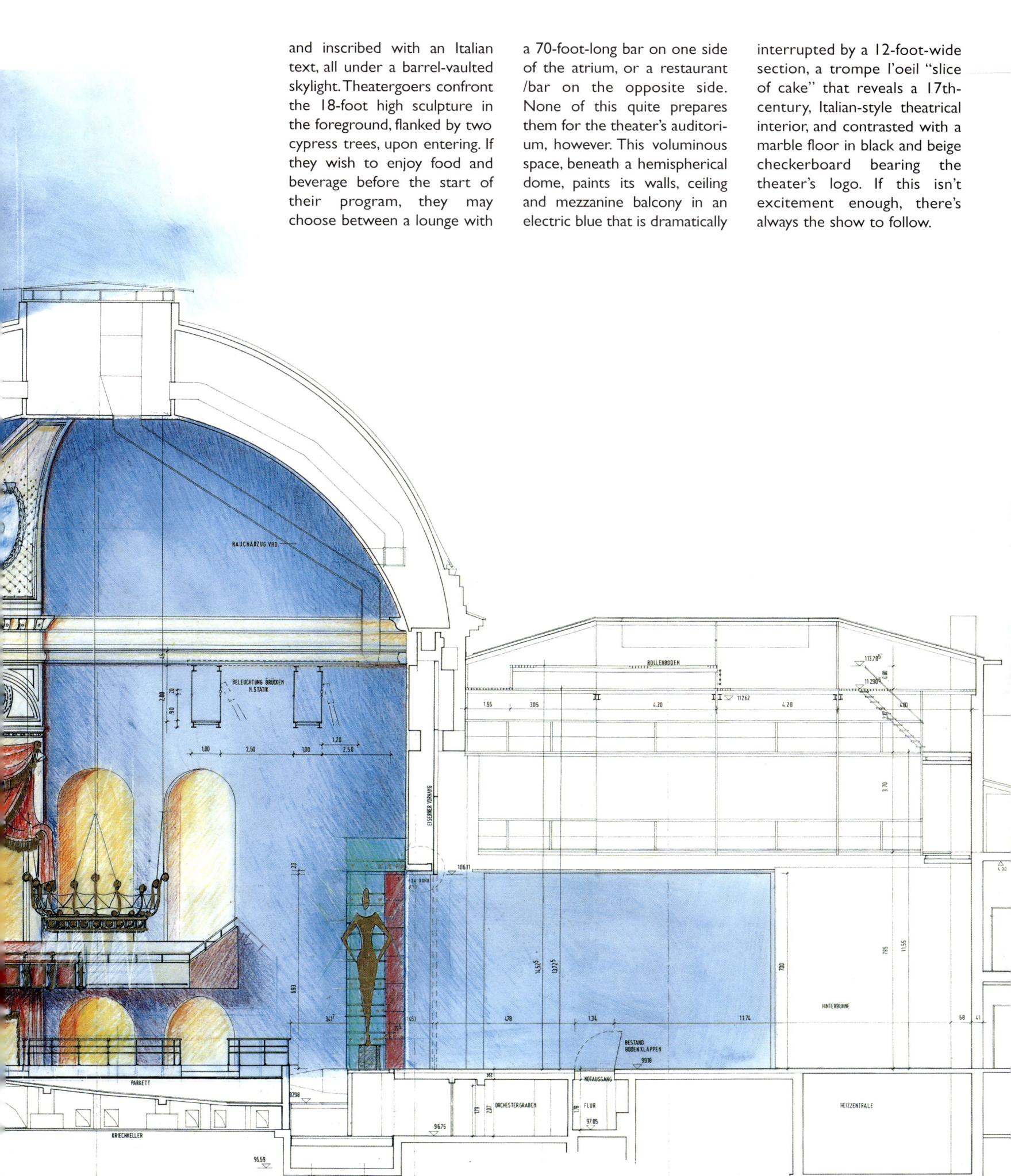

Upper: Bar at lounge.
Lower: Bar at restaurant/bar.
Opposite above: Individual sculpture.
Opposite below: Auditorium showing marble floor.

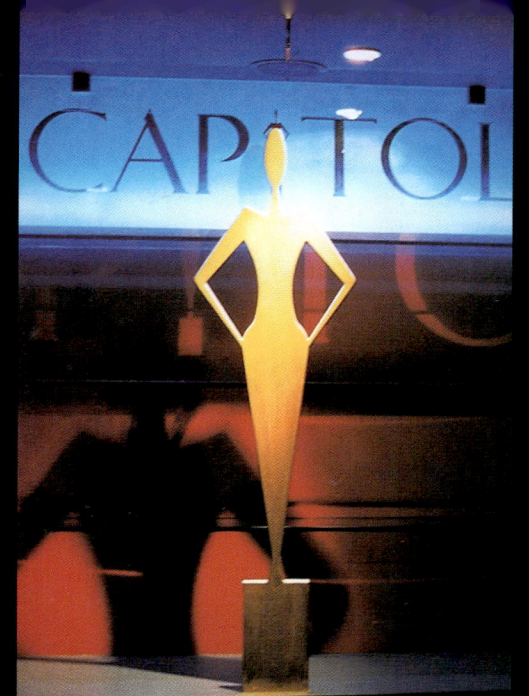

Bulova
Queens, New York, USA

Time doesn't stand still at the former watch factory in Queens, New York known as Bulova Corporate Center. A dominant, Art Moderne-style landmark along New York's Grand Central Parkway since 1953, the 450,000-square-foot structure emerged as a class A office building after an extensive 1988 renovation that included its vast, central atrium. Since that time, the building's tenants have been enjoying the atrium as 10:10, the 350-seat Bulova New York Restaurant. The name refers to the time used to set clocks for photography, and is just one of many elements in the beautifully detailed design by Jean-Pierre Heim with Tyrone Roper, architect, and Suzan Blumenfeld, interior designer. that refer to time symbolically. For example, the plan outlines the shape of a wristwatch with circulation aisles leading to the centrally located bar, which is portrayed as a clock face. As the focal point of the restaurant, the bar is crafted like an exquisite timepiece, tracing back-lighted Roman numerals on a 30-foot diameter circular soffit that is reflected by the circular bar countertop and the circular

Upper: Entry portico.
Lower: Portico upper level.
Opposite: Centrally located bar.
Overleaf: Floor plan, design studies and central spatial zone.

pattern of black granite on the floor. The three-part composition of the building's entry portico serves as an additional thematic motif, so indoor porticos repeat the proportions of the exterior portico at the same time they spatially define and acoustically separate 10:10's dining zones. Each zone, in turn, is supported by its own service bar, featuring a countertop, handrails and trim in stainless steel that resemble clock components. Large trompe l'oeil paintings intensify the ambiance by depicting universal themes about time and history. One painting combines images of stairs, water, desert, classical architecture and a clock set at 10:10 in a composition that has become the signature image for the restaurant's menu and advertisements. Two other trompe l'oeil paintings, placed on either side of the largest of seven working clocks on display, project very different moods: one portrays the building's portico half buried in sand, and the other shows the portico facing a stormy sky with its clock set at an early morning hour, anticipating the sunrise. The seven clocks are impressive in their own right, reminding customers that fine timepieces can be seen as decorative elements as well as useful machines. And there's nothing to prevent customers from using them to keep track of the global economy, or to schedule their next restaurant reservations--at least in the time zones for London, Paris, Rome, Sydney, Tokyo, Los Angeles and New York.

Above: Maitre d'hotel station.
Right: Rendering of central spatial zone.

Club Med
Dakar, Senegal, Africa

Theme park holidays are not for everyone, which is why Club Med guests have chosen to vacation at its authentic, low-key facilities in exotic locales for over 50 years. As part of a global rejuvenation program of some 70 facilities for Club Med, Jean-Pierre Heim created a fascinating African experience for guests staying at the hotelier's existing, 30-year-old, 450-bed seaside resort just outside Dakar, Senegal in 2000, that draws on native art, materials and craftsmanship to work its charm. Having designed numerous hotels, including a Club Med in Morocco, Heim has taken advantage of his familiarity with both hotel development and African culture to produce an exceptional transformation that has included site analysis, surveying and programming as well as planning, architecture, interior design and the design of all furnishings for this resort on the westernmost geographic point of West Africa. Of course, the project has been aided immeasurably by a tropical landscape resplendent with coconut

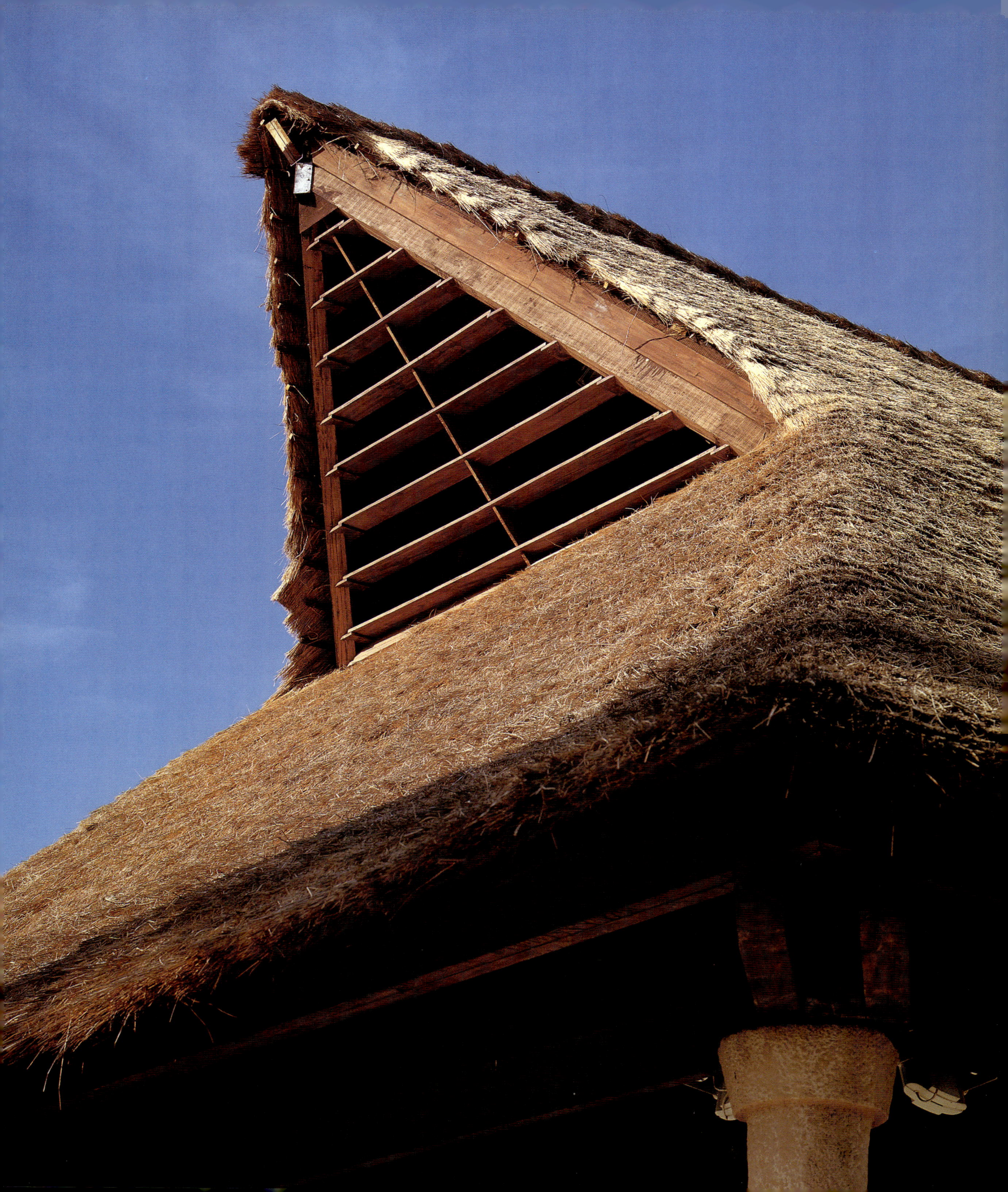

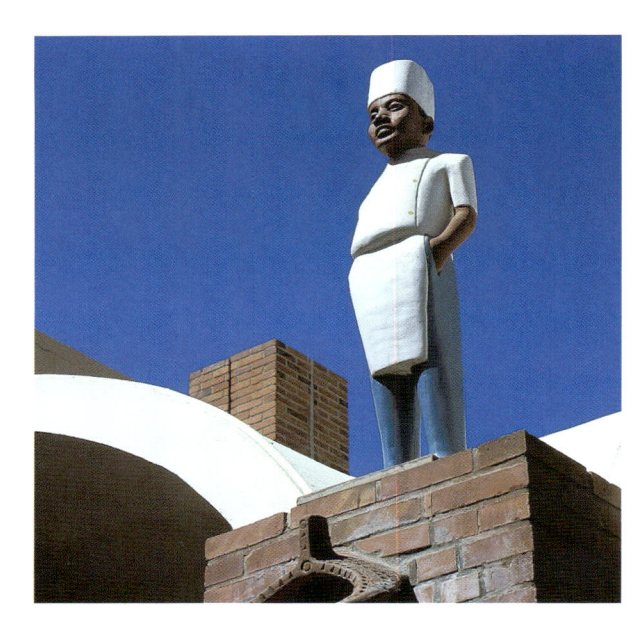

This page: Two examples of locally handcrafted furnishings and art.
Opposite: Entrance to a new gift shop.

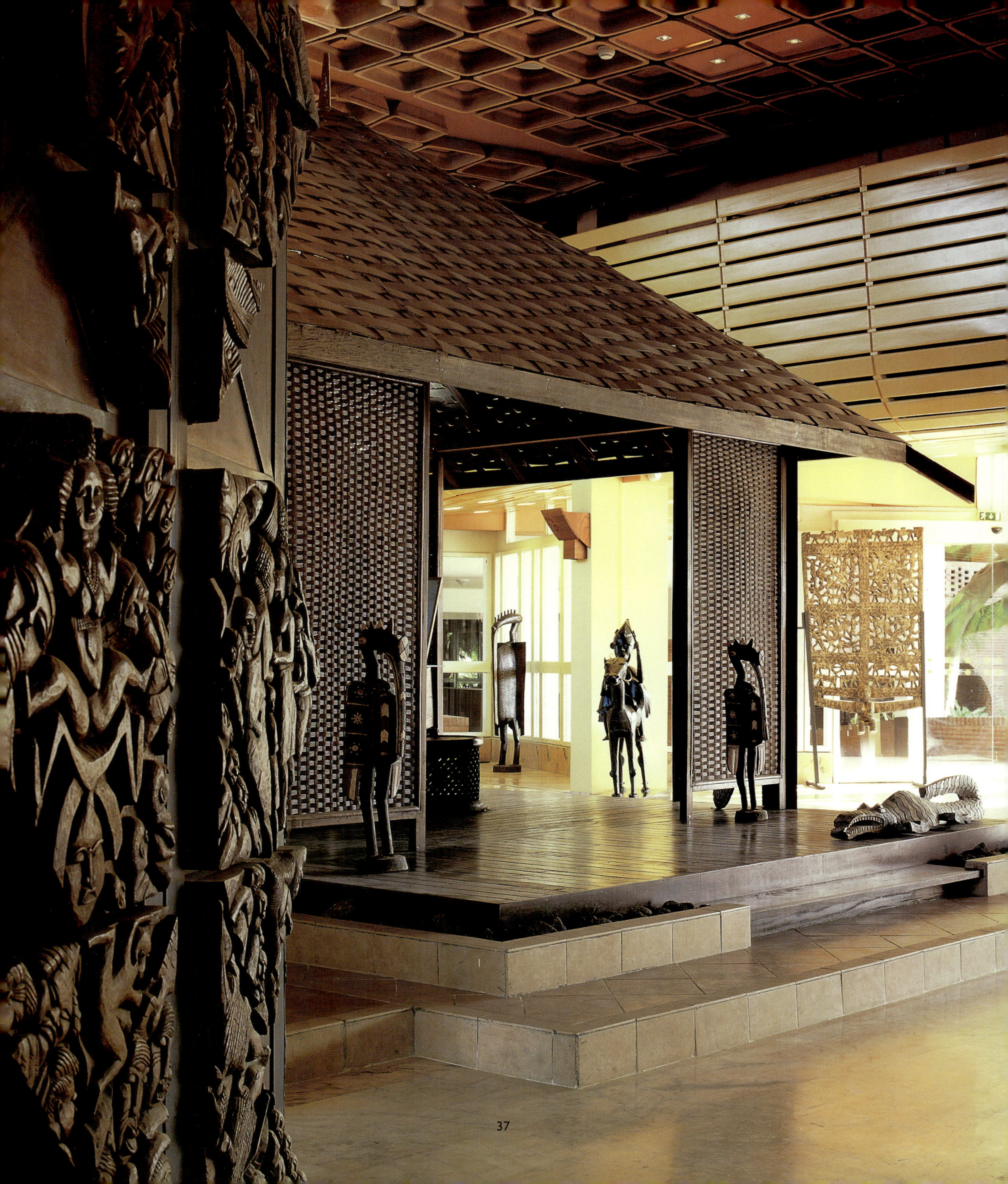

Above and right: Native art and dramatic lighting transform a corridor into an art gallery.
Far right: Registration counter and concierge desk.

palms, and a seashore offering a tableau of white sand and black volcanic rock. With such natural splendors as a backdrop, Heim's fresh ideas are visible not only in guestrooms, lobby, four restaurants, bars, circulation and a new gift shop, but also in such reconfigured exterior zones as a theater, poolside bars and restaurants, — including a spectacular new pool built virtually by hand — plus two new buildings, a single-story, 900-seat restaurant and a hut-like palapa for the all-important main bar. What guests will not see is the extensive and coordinated effort sustaining the renovation. Almost 1,200 workers participated in the on-site construction alone, laboring under every conceivable weather condition, day and night, with and without modern devices, and following local techniques whenever possible. In the end, tradition and the modern world coexist amicably in the distinctive milieu that has emerged. The locally made furnishings — including all bedroom furniture, produced in the factories of village craftsmen — European products, and one-of-a-kind pieces Heim has obtained at bazaars and other native sources throughout the Ivory Coast weave a palpable spell throughout Club Med in Dakar, conjuring an enchanted world where air conditioning, fax machines, televisions and other latter-day conveniences do not seem out of placing sharing the Senegal sun.

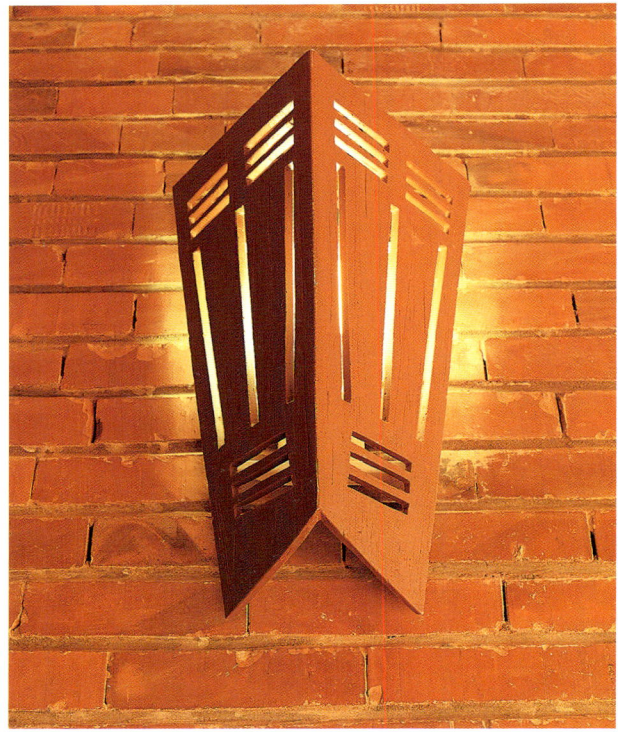

This page: Lighting fixtures designed by Jean-Pierre Heim.
Opposite: The bedroom ensemble evokes Senegalese culture.

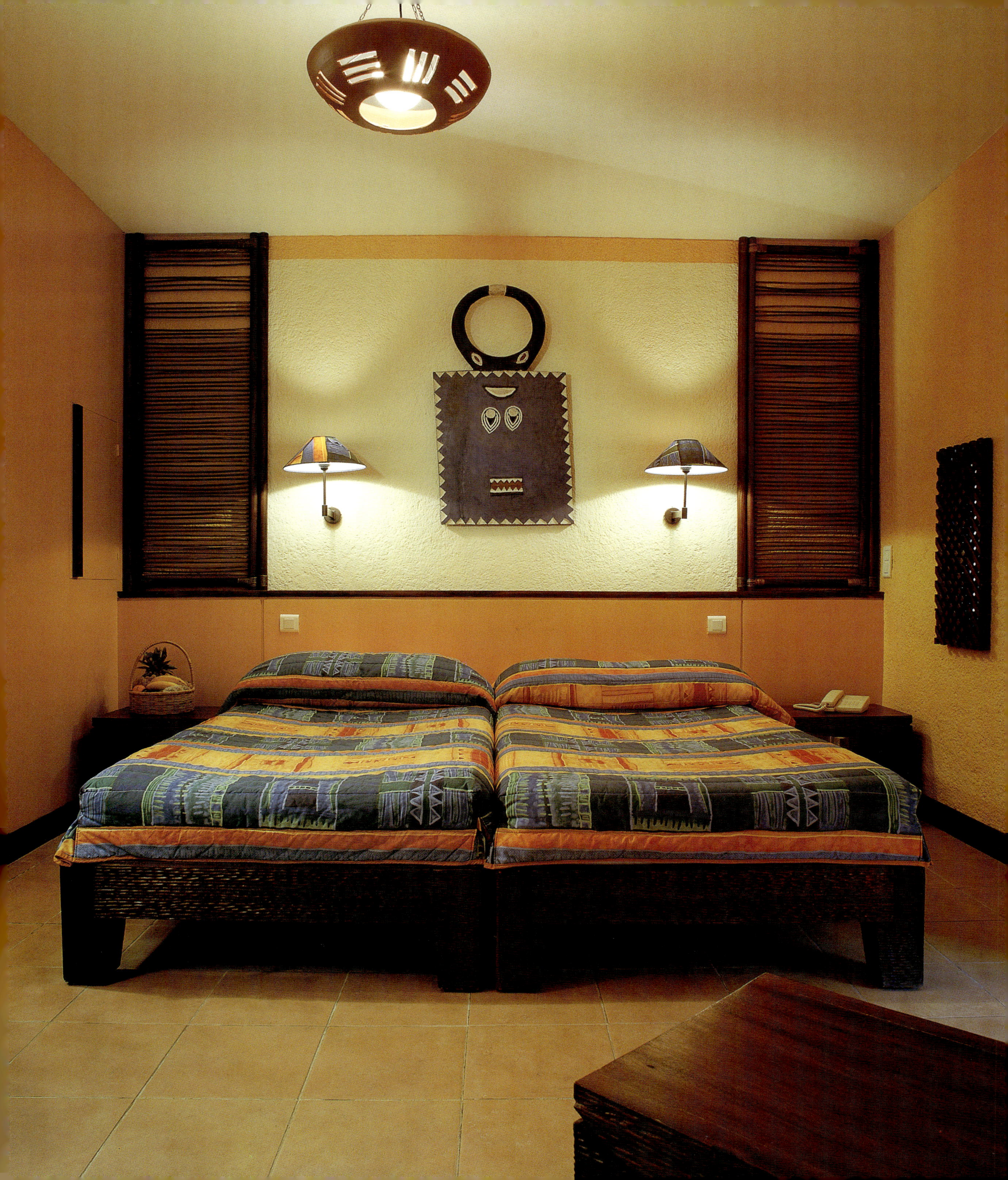

DIMANCHE - SUNDAY
THEME - DRESS CODE
BLANC / WHITE
18H00 MUSIQUE CLASSIQUE
CLASSICAL MUSIC
19H15 JEUX AU BAR /
20H00 BUFFET LES ALMADIES
21H30 PISTE DE DANSE / DANCE FLOOR
22H00 SPECTACLE / SHOW
" TITANIC "

43

This page and opposite: Arches provide a strong leitmotif
in the highly detailed interiors for registration and food service.

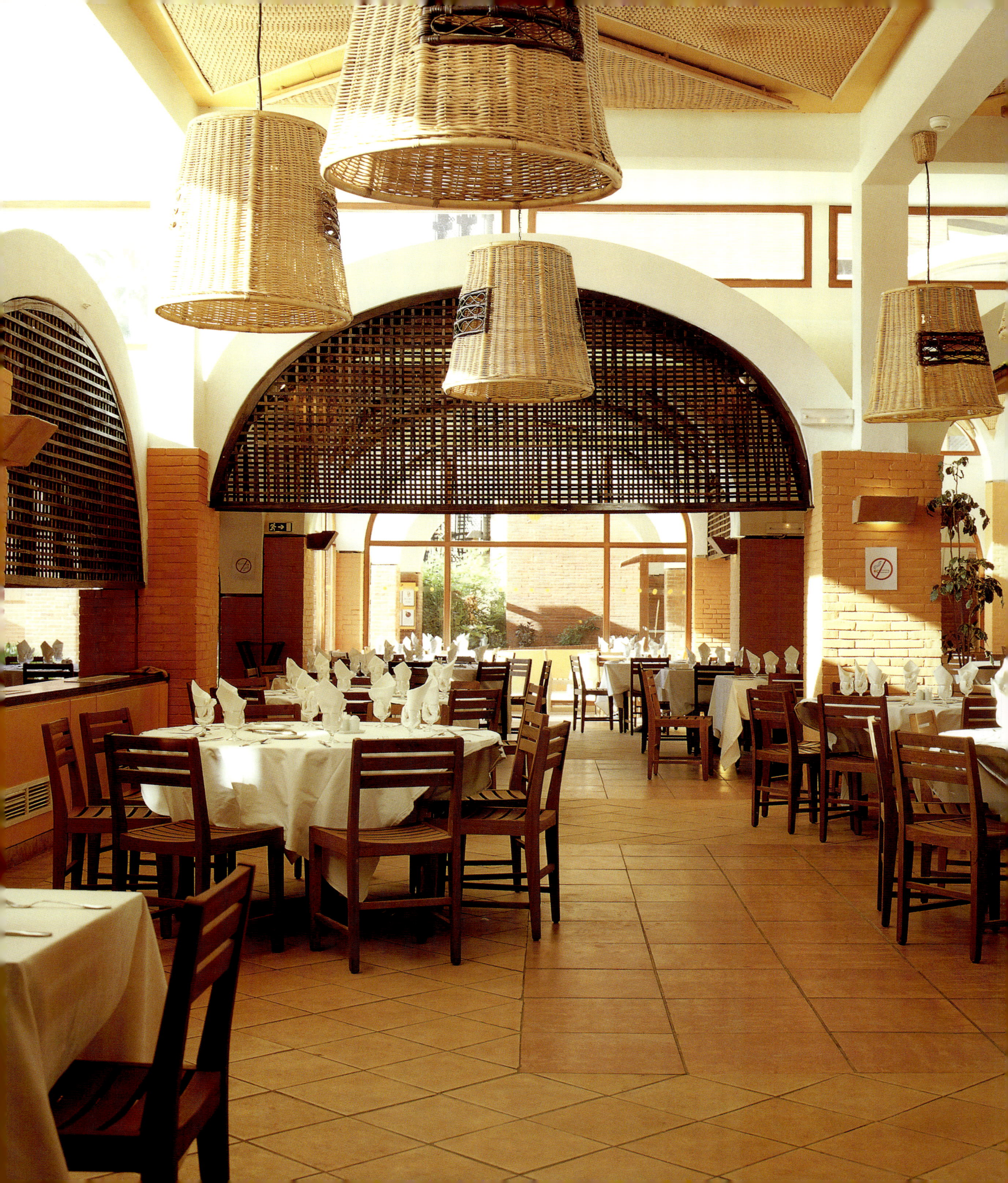

Luxor Palace

Dresden, Germany

Wars, fires, floods and political intrigue have threatened the heritage of Dresden, the magnificent capital of Saxony on the Elbe River, but they have never prevented the city from preserving and restoring such cultural treasures as its splendid Renaissance, Baroque and 19th century architecture, including the Zwinger Palace, Semper Opera House and Frauenkirche. So the recent rebirth of a nine-story, 22,000-square foot commercial structure, transforming what was built by the Russians in 1958 into a modern, mixed-use facility, continues a Dresden tradition. However, the design of two major spaces in the structure by Jean-Pierre Heim, the Luxor

This page: Painted frieze above the Luxor Palace bar.
Opposite: Interior stairs of the Luxor Palace.

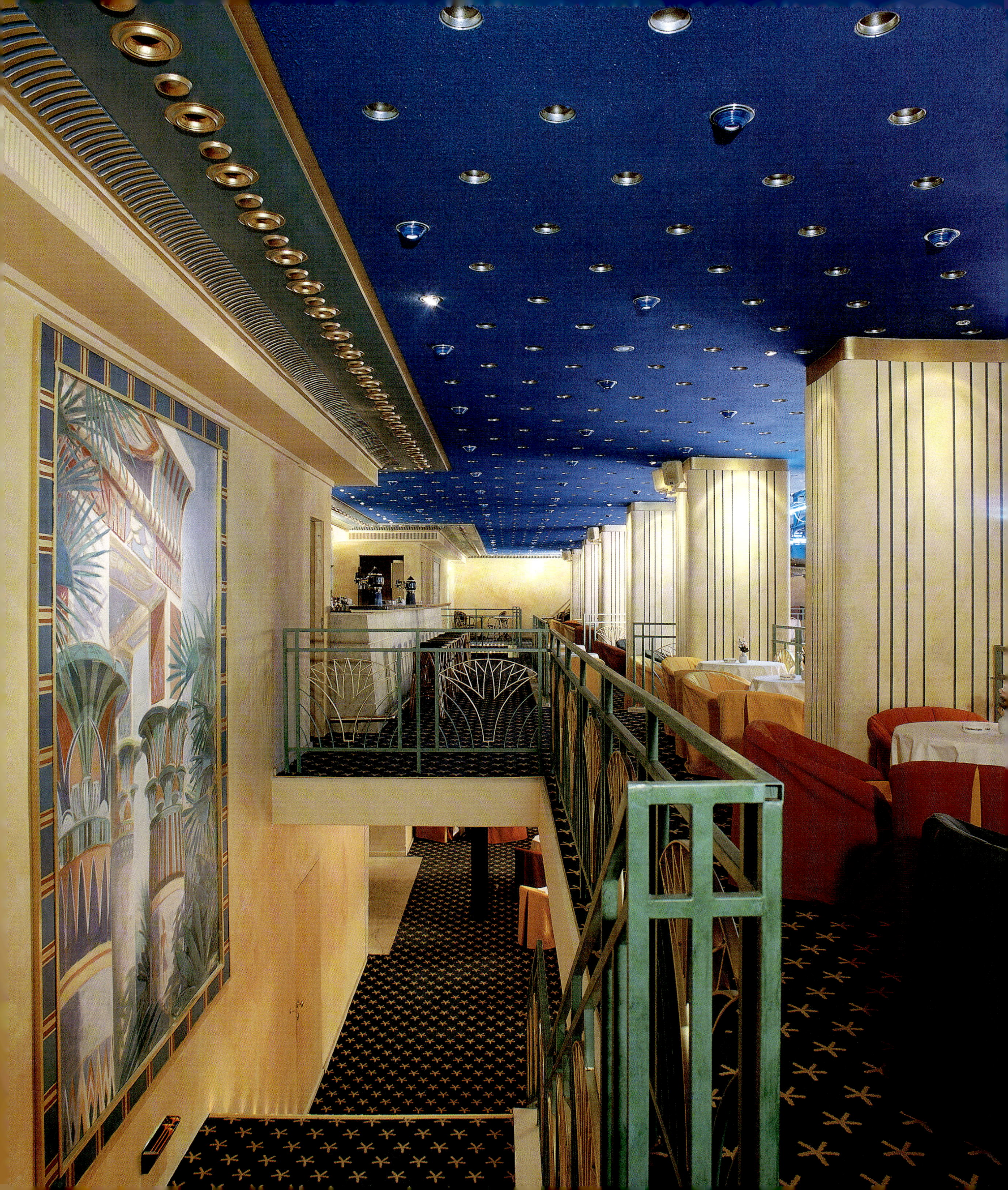

Palace, a 400-seat restaurant that doubles as a music/dance hall on weekends, and the Sphinx Cafe, a 100-seat, street level coffee shop, has broken fresh ground in the ancient city. Asked by the building's owners to create a distinctive hospitality complex on the lower levels to complement new office and residential space on the upper levels, Heim saw the 6,000 square feet of raw space--reduced to bare columns on black granite floors--as a surreal reminder of ancient Egyptian temples and pyramids. His insight has flowered into a dramatic and appealing environment that would probably have startled the Russians. The project began with the construction of a double-height mezzanine that raised the floor area to 8,500 square feet, followed by the insertion of a grand stairway ascending from the street level to the top floors. Into this revived architectural shell, Heim has placed two independent but compatible facilities whose visual strength comes from both the skillful manipulation of space, playing on the meticulously symmetrical and relentlessly processional nature of Egyptian architecture, and the careful detailing of interior forms and surfaces, marshaling the talents of such French suppliers of building materials, furnishings and artisan skills as Design Connection International, Heim's own producer of furniture and graphics, to add the finishing decorative touches. The results, as shown in the lively and informal dining space of the Sphinx Cafe and the ravishingly formal restaurant, dance floor, bar and lounge of the Luxor Palace, have been impressive enough to wow the Dresden public and win design awards. Will Dresden now add Egyptian Revival to its inventory of architectural styles? The Luxor Palace is a fine first step.

This page: An intimate corner displaying meticulous decoration.
Opposite: Restaurant with new mezzanine added.

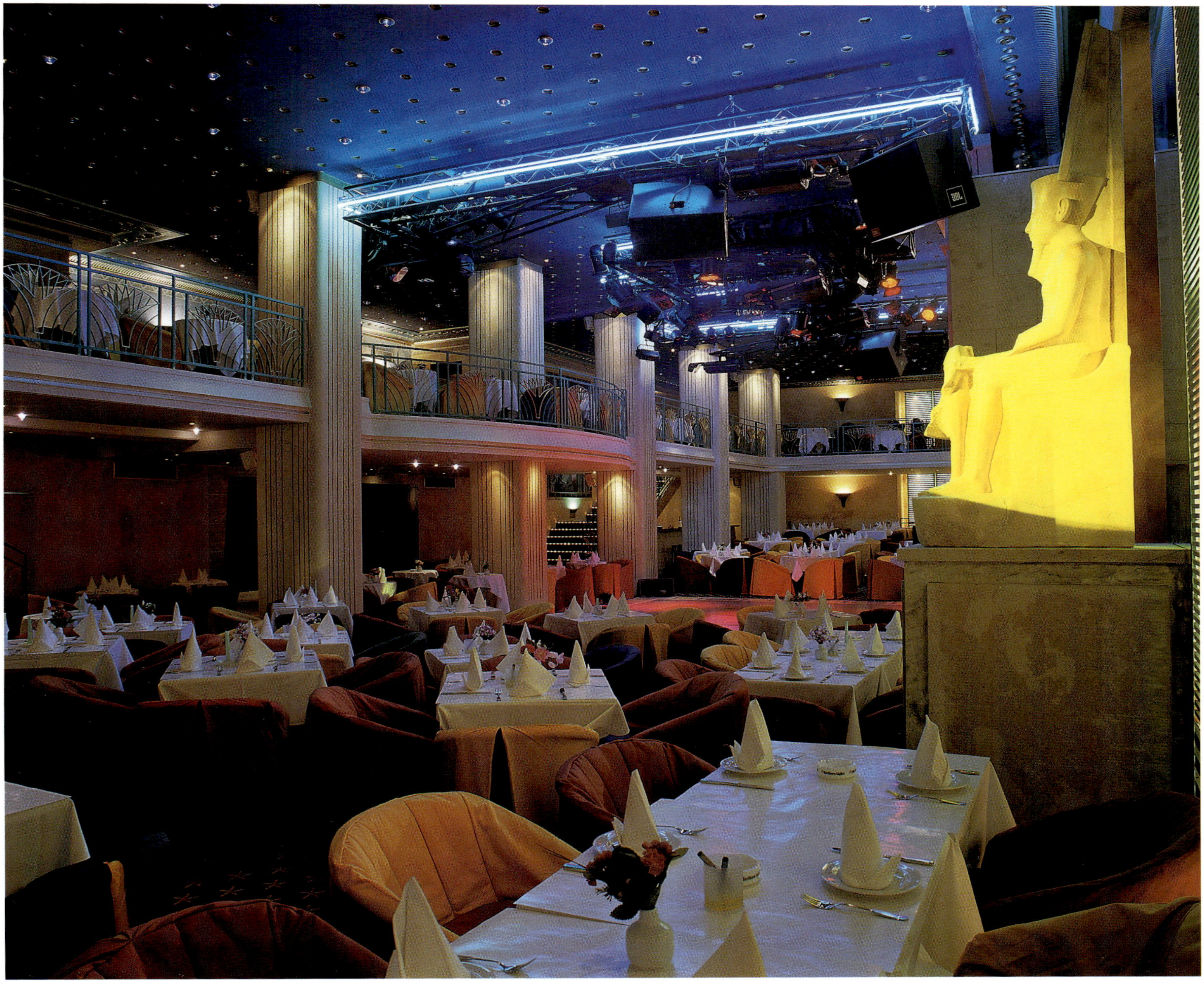

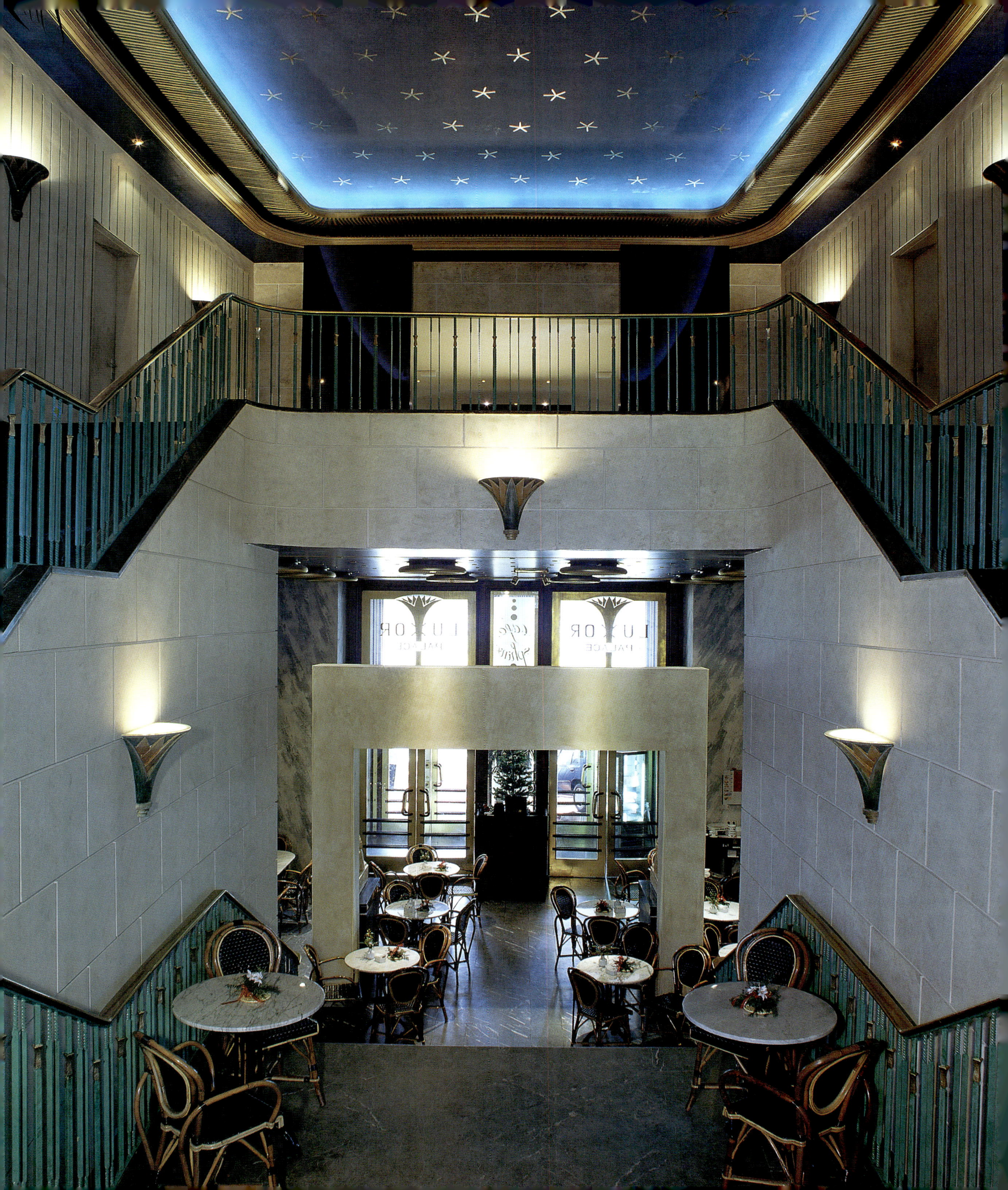

This page: An exquisitely detailed entrance, captured in masonry, carpet, textiles and lighting.
Opposite: Looking from the Luxor Palace to the Cafe Sphinx on the street level, with downtown Dresden
Following pages: Examples of the high quality of decorative work achieved for the Cafe Sphinx and Luxor Palace.

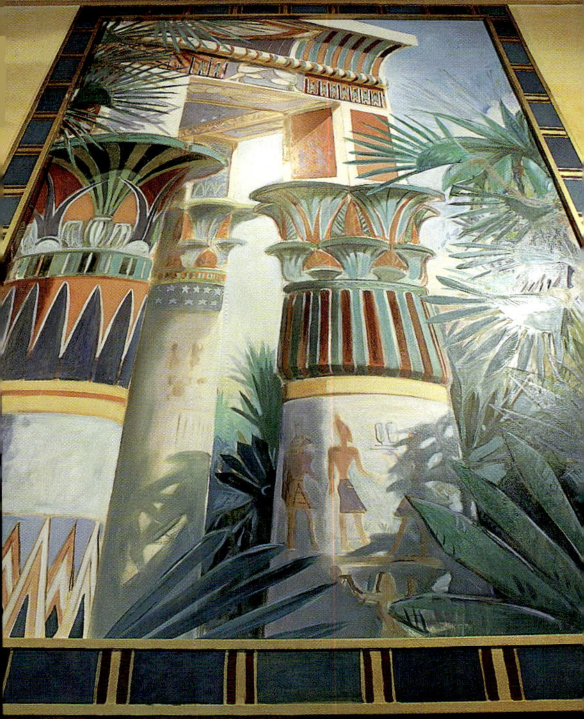

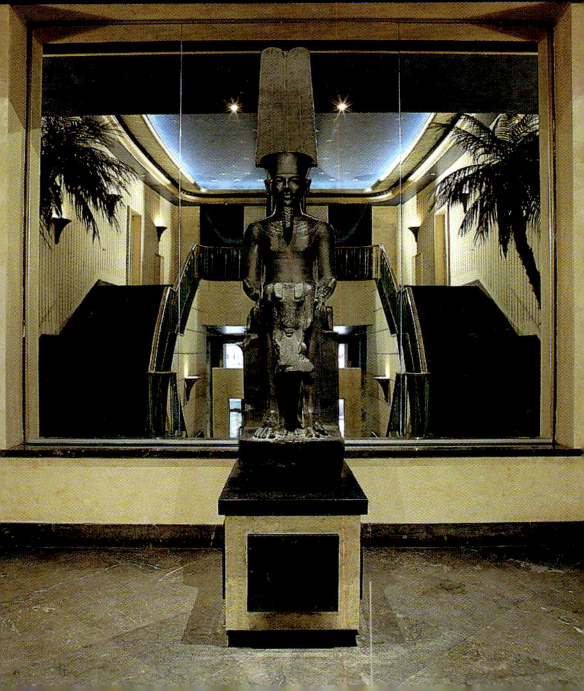

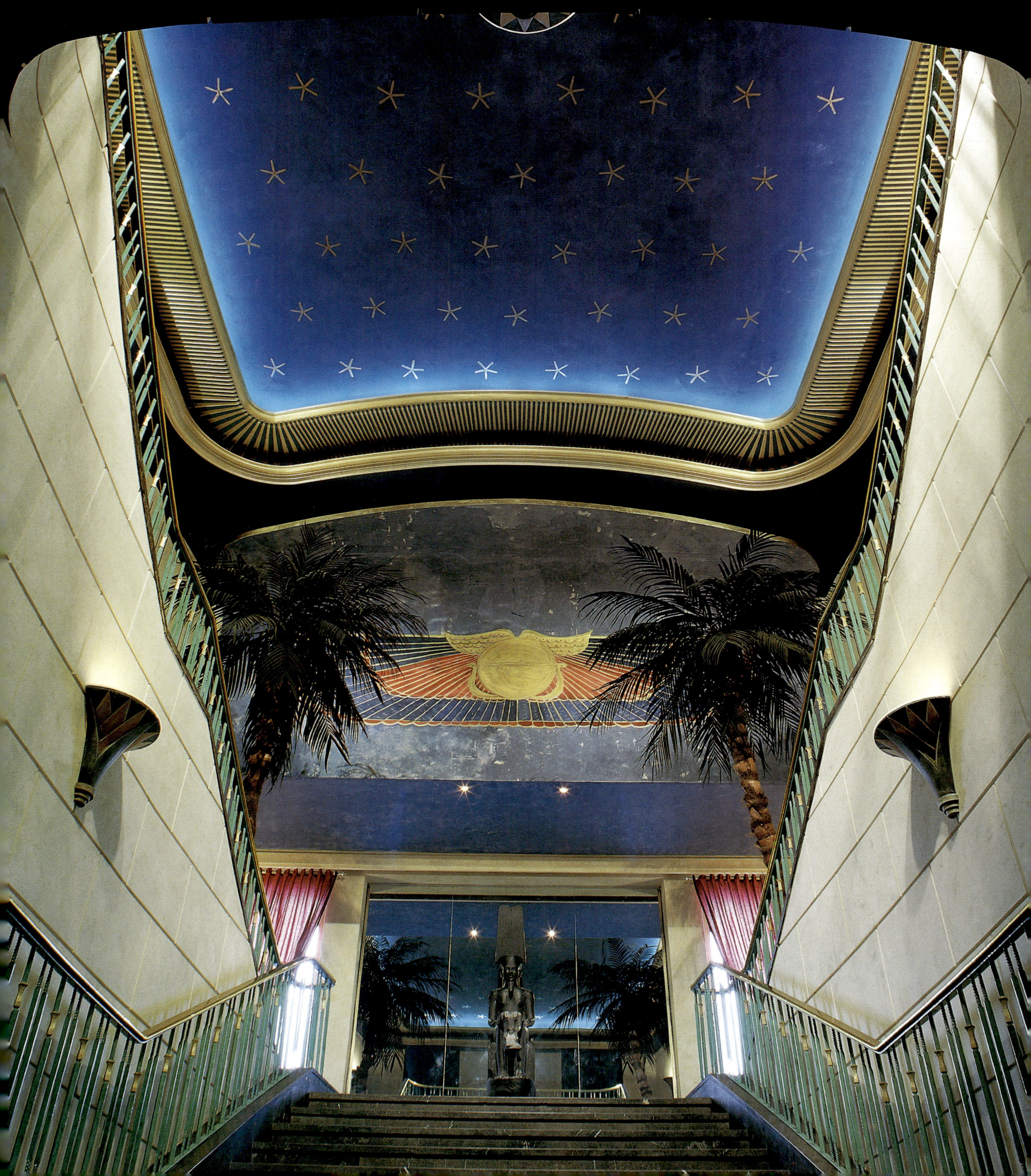

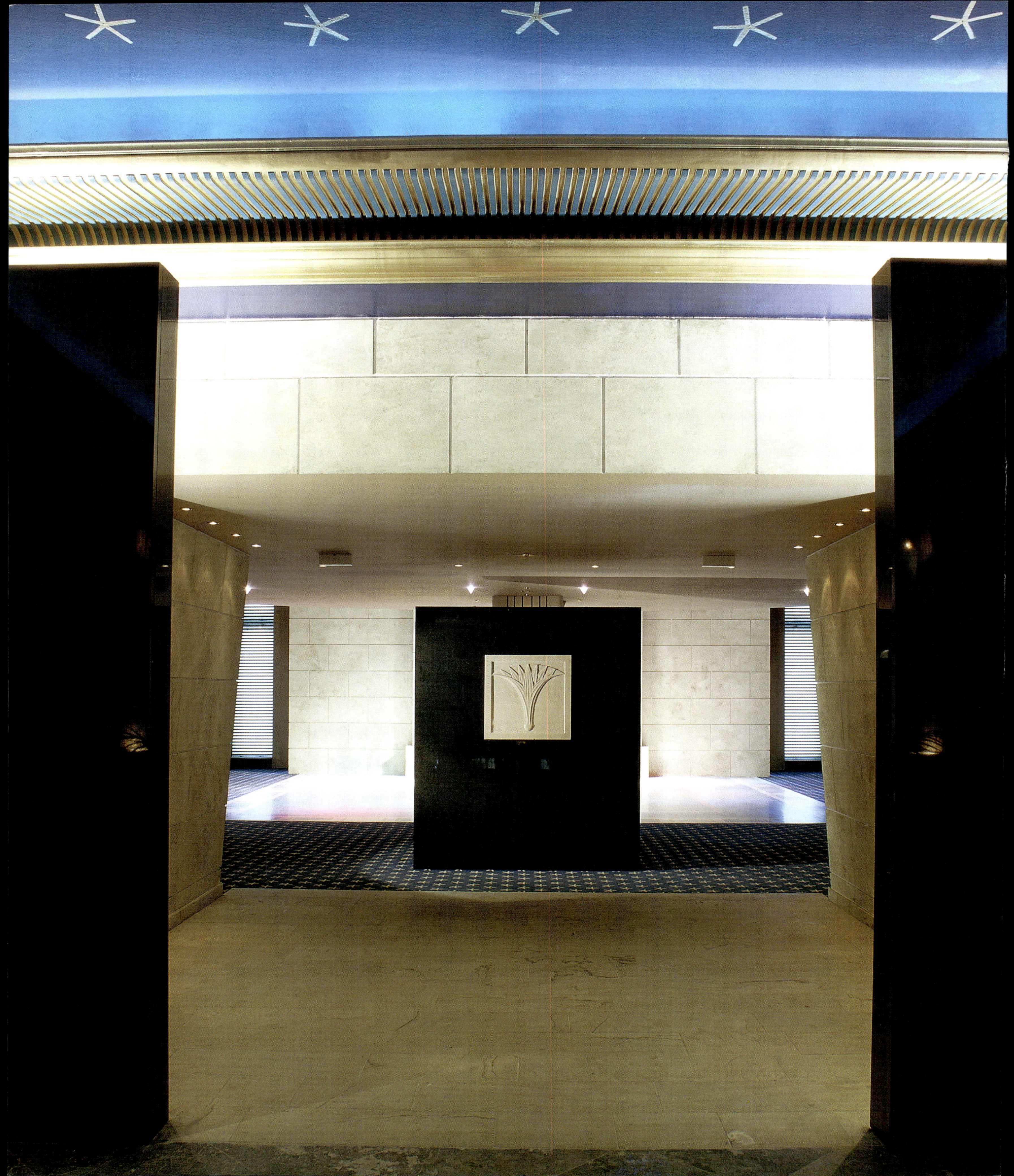

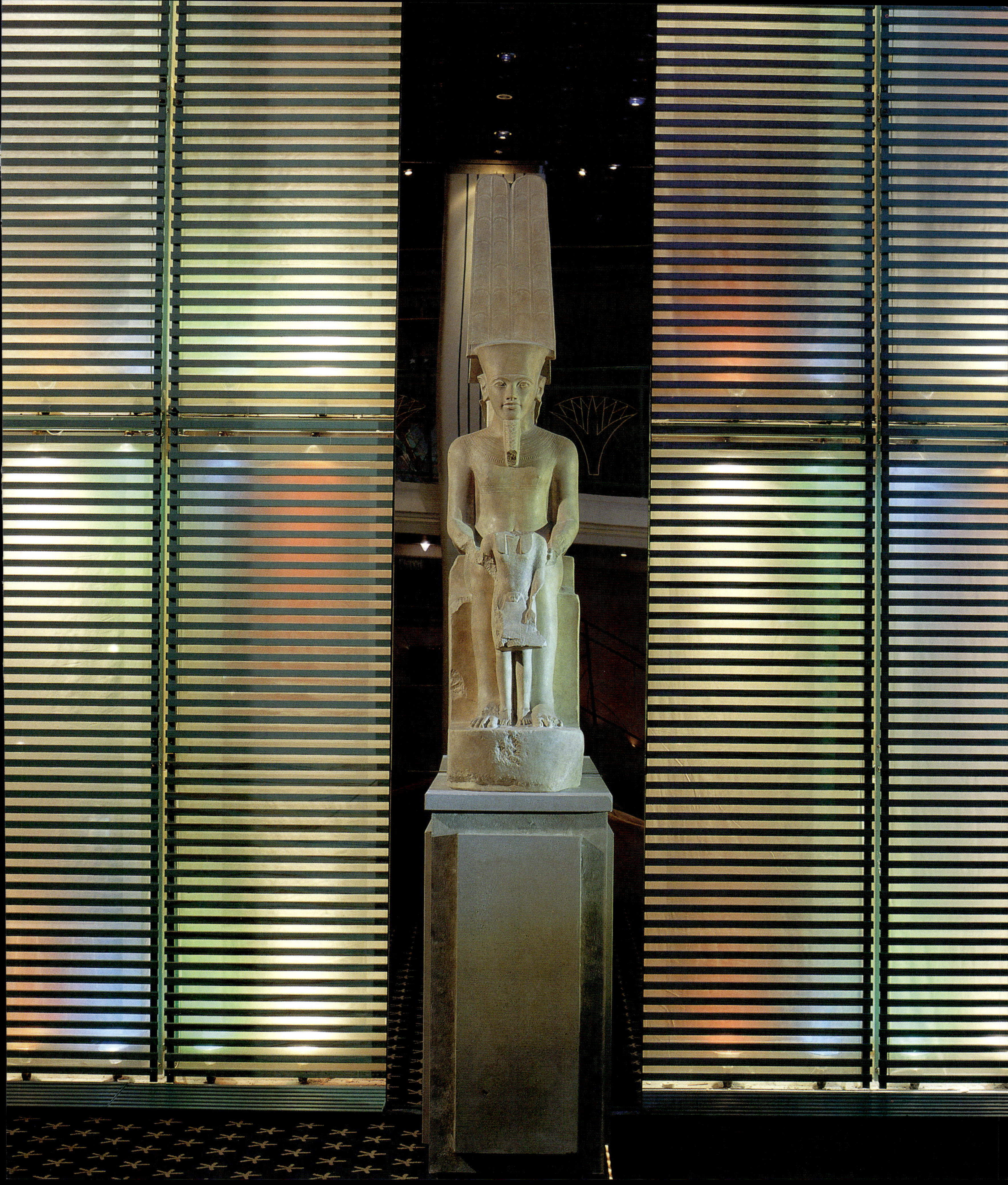

Luxor Cinema

Paris, France

Newly finished and unabashedly opulent movie palaces were contributing their luminosity to the City of Light in 1921, the year Pathé, a pioneer in movie theaters that still plays a leading role in the industry. The glory of this Egyptian-themed cinema, located at 170 boulevard Magenta and known to movie goers as the Louxor, would not last after World War II, when it became a ballroom where jazz bands performed. Nevertheless, the Louxor has endured every change, remaining closed for now but boasting a facade sufficiently intact to be designated as a landmark by the local historical building commission. Since the auditorium of the Louxor can hold as many as 1,100 spectators, Jean-Pierre Heim proposed a project in 1994 that addresses all the concerns of landmark preservation in converting the building to a center for cinema, retailing and fine dining. The project would include such features as a small private reception and cinema theater in the basement, a museum store to sell books and gifts based on ancient Egyptian history, such as objects from the Egyptian collection at the Louvre, a coffee bar and a comfortable, 900-seat theater with advanced technology for cinema and live performances. A cigar bar named "les cigars du Pharaon" would be located on the mezzanine, while a 200-seat restaurant and bar would occupy the terrace, overlooking the city from a newly constructed space with a 15-foot-high ceiling. The restored facade would bring back the original colors of the glazed terra cotta frescoes, as well as the sign at the top and the huge billboard to the side, proclaiming to the surrounding neighborhood that its venerable Louxor has returned.

This page: Terra cotta details to be restored.
Opposite: Facade after historic preservation.

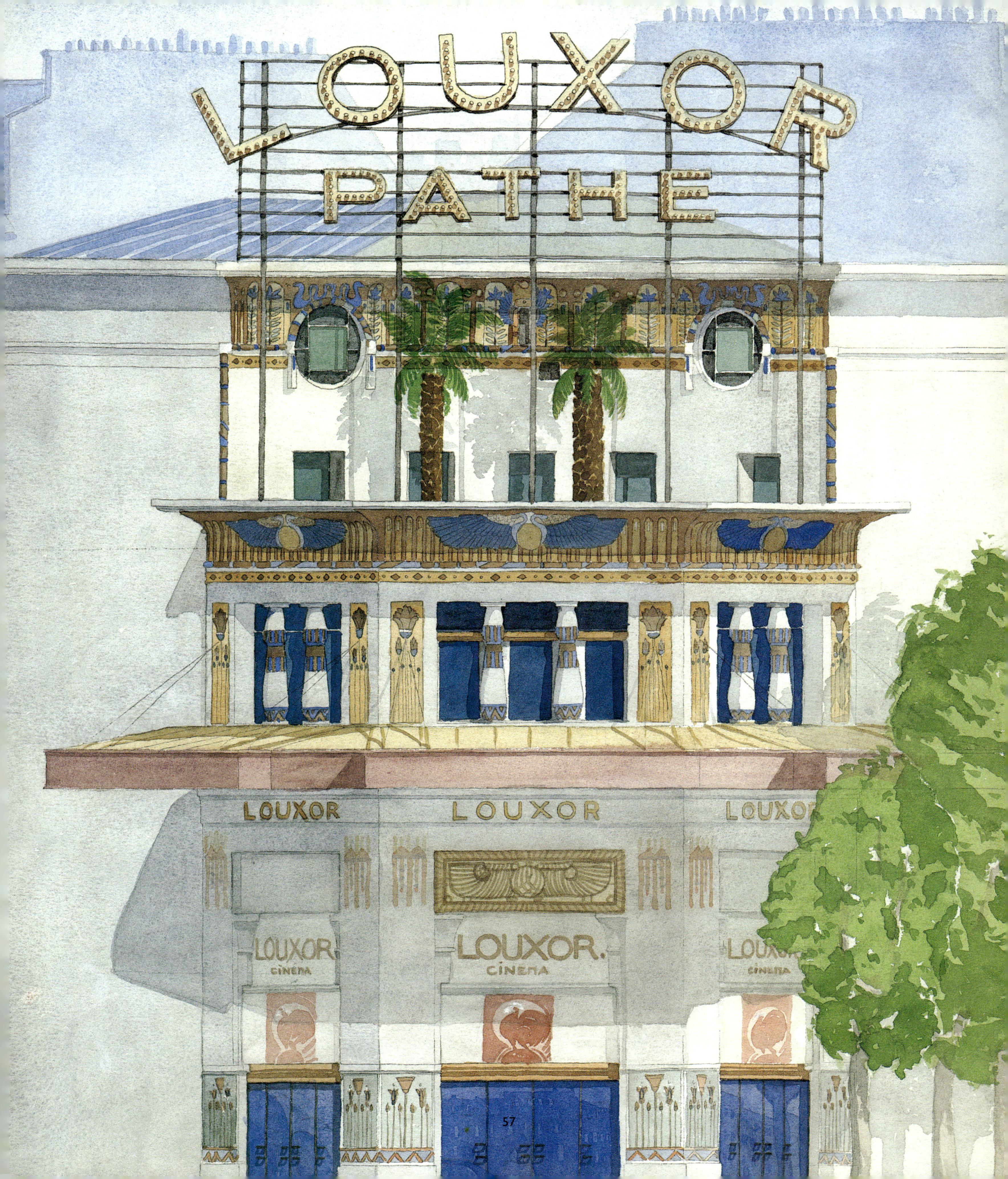
LOUXOR
PATHE
LOUXOR
LOUXOR
LOUXOR
CINEMA
LOUXOR.
CINEMA

Cinepanorama

Greece

Combining an ancient architectural form with specially adapted, state-of-the-art technologies produces Cinepanorama, a multi-functional theater conceived by Jean-Pierre Heim in 2003 for a Grecian archeological site or other prime tourist attraction. Its architecture is timeless Minimalist. The square, U-shaped structure of stone walls and a tensile fabric roof shelters 400 people, and the landscaped amphitheater, descending from the square structure to a giant screen rising from the base of the amphitheater, seats several hundred more. More than a cinema, it is also a venue for theater, music, conferences, weddings and other private events, restaurant and bar. Greece, as a popular vacation destination blessed with blue skies nine months each year, would be the right host for this unique project, during the 2004 Olympics and long after.

This page: The square structure seen at grade.
Opposite: The amphitheater.
Overleaf: Site plan with giant screen.

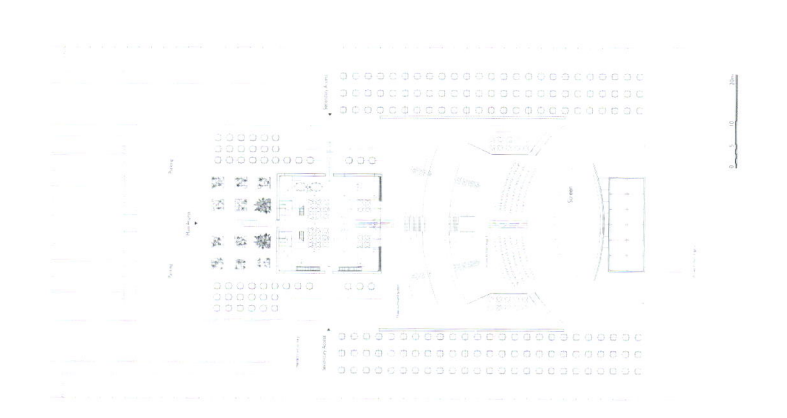

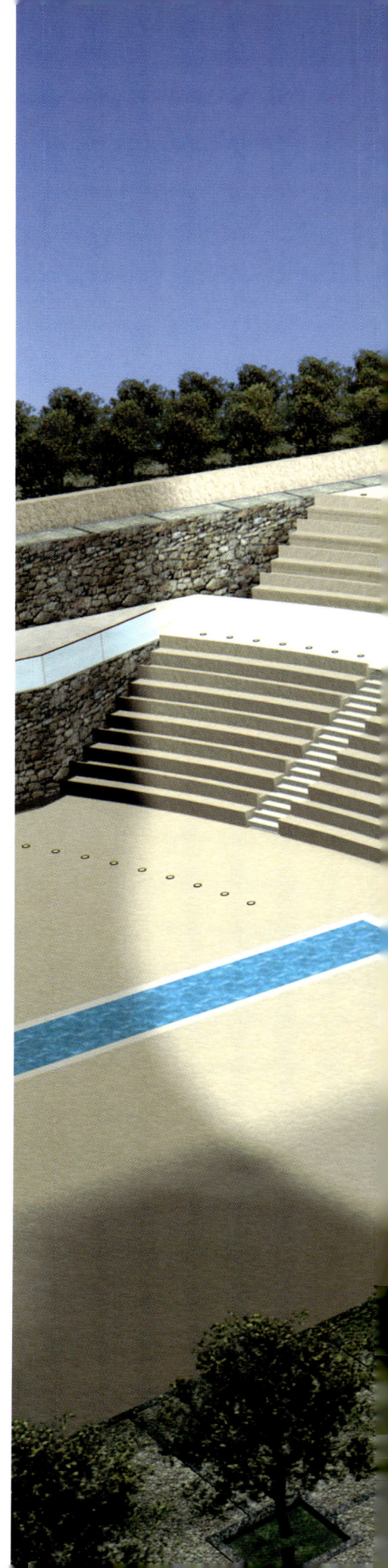

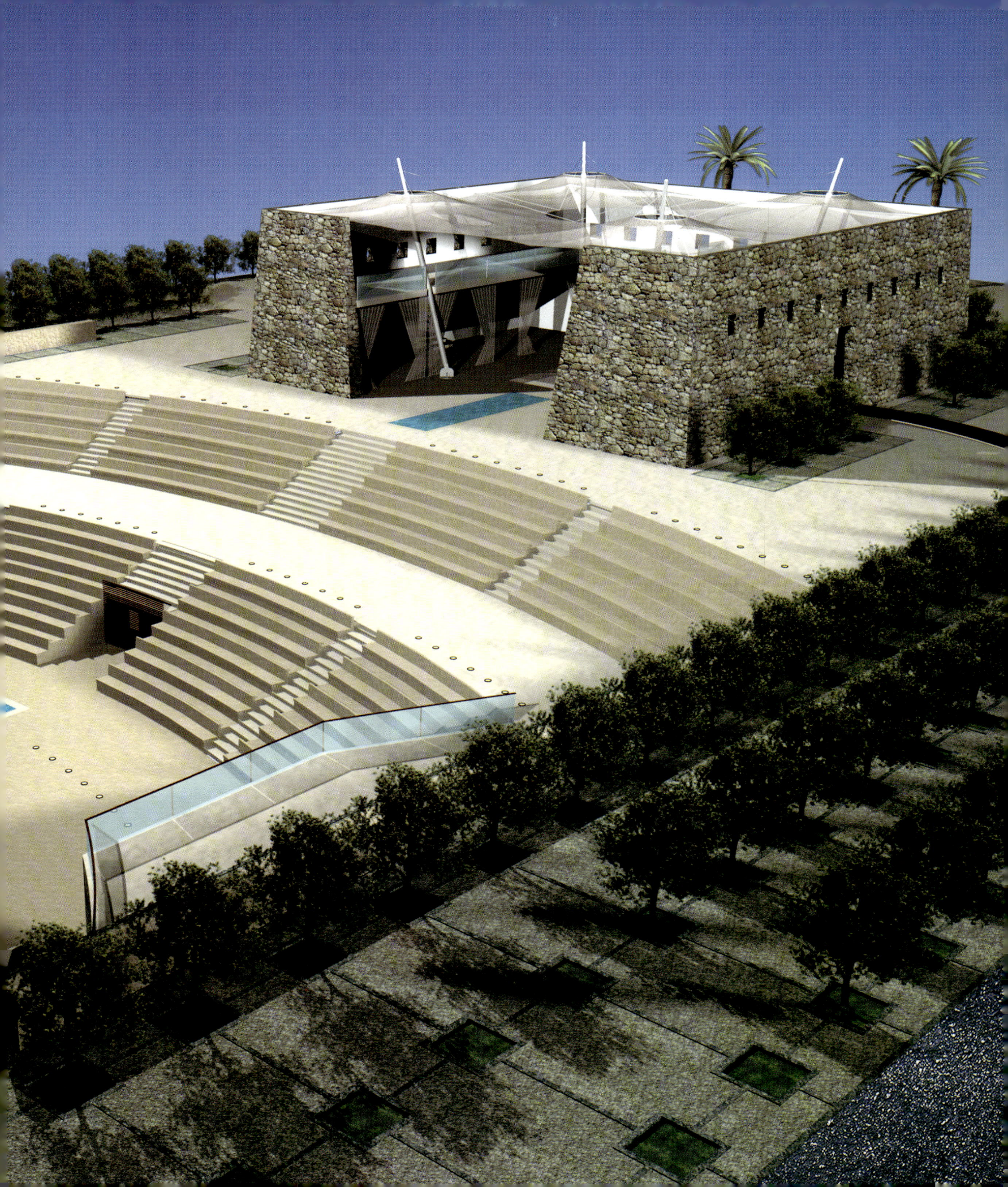

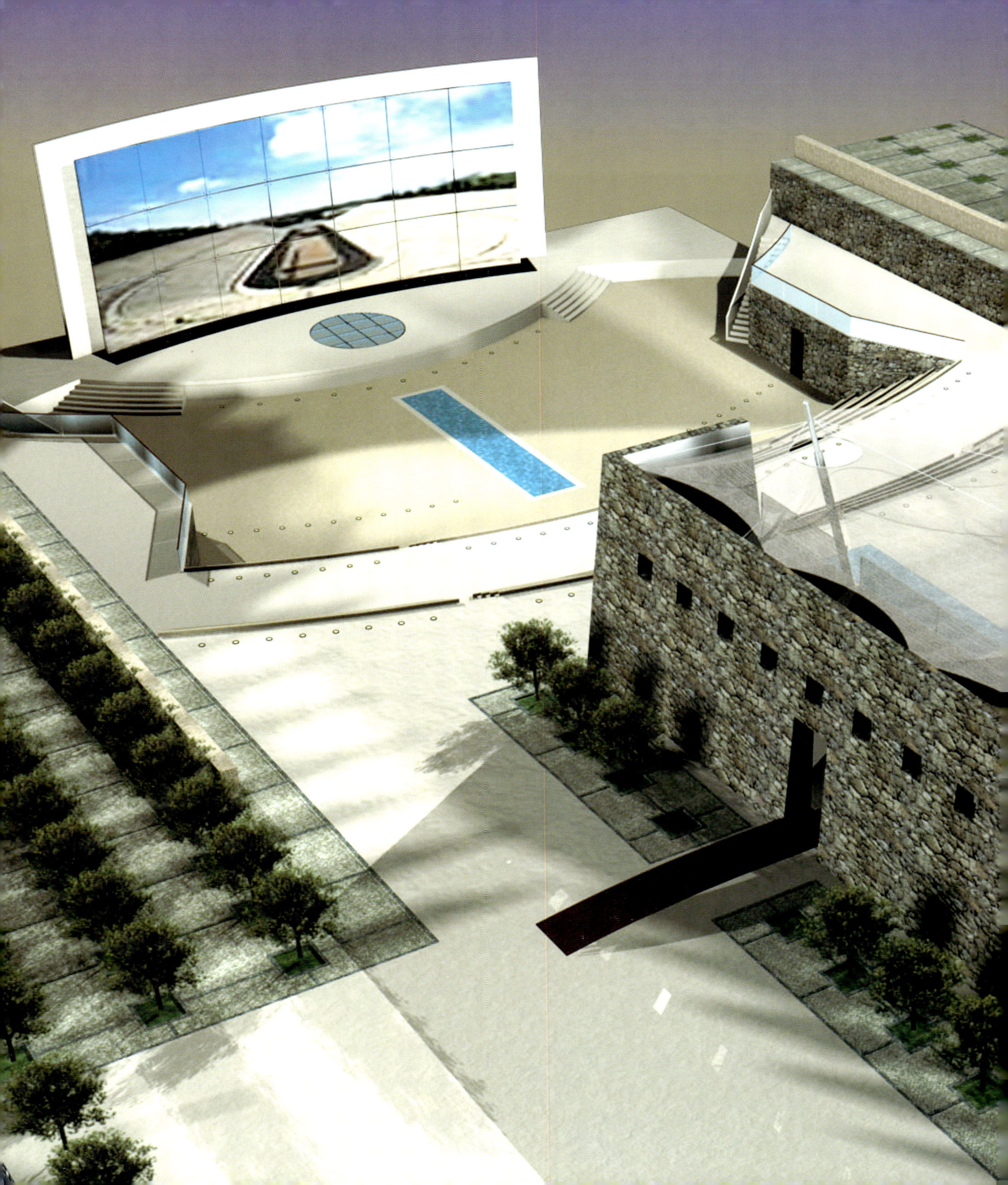

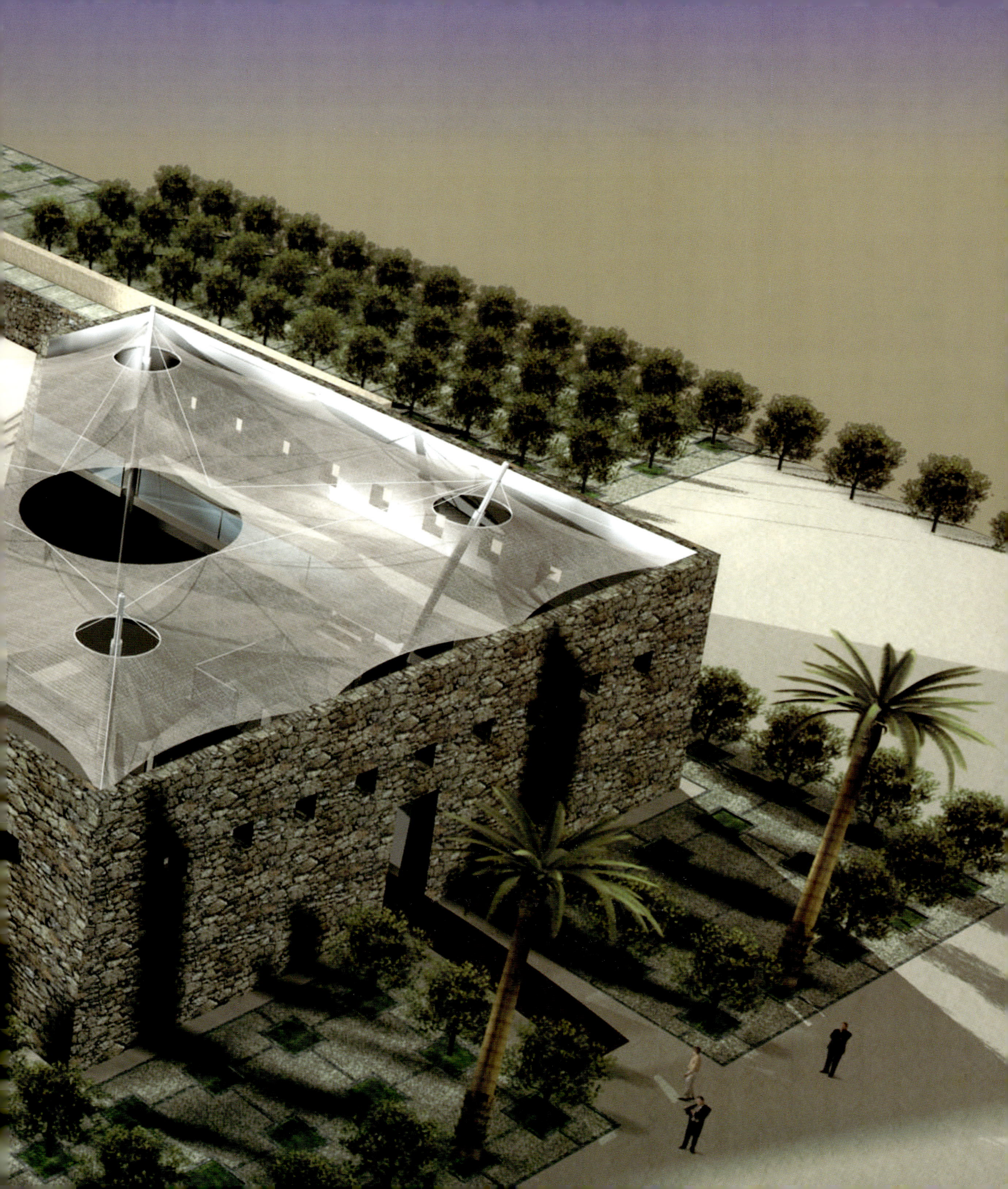

Chameleon

Frankfurt, Germany

Night life may not be what most visitors associate with Frankfurt, the historic birthplace of Goethe, financial and commercial capital of Germany, seat of the nation's leading stock exchange and home of the European Central Bank. Yet the city's rich cultural life fosters considerable diversity, making ample room for such lively gathering places as Chameleon, a 2,000-square foot nightclub designed by Jean-Pierre Heim in 1990. Housed in a vaulted basement beneath Die Leiter, an existing restaurant designed by Jean-Pierre Heim in 1982, the club functions as a discotheque and after-hours restaurant. A long, crescent-shaped bar, situated at the heart of the floor plan and visible from everywhere, functions as the hinge that links all the disparate spaces. It is accompanied by a monumental portico at the back of the dance floor, which guests see framed by a vaulted opening the moment they enter, as the interior's secondary focus. The nightclub's name serves as a leitmotif and suitable metaphor for the lighting design, which is used to alter the mood of the spaces. Except for accent lighting directed down to the bar counter, other lighting is indirect and designed specifically for the bar soffit, the dance floor and the ceiling vaults. Yet fixed points of reference are generously distributed to tell guests where they are. The horizontally layered walls, for example, include a granite base, a stainless steel and painted metal wainscot, an eye-level band of mirror and a lighting soffit above that wrap around the nightclub like a belt and act as lines of reference to unify areas of varying distances and heights. A number of well-known design devices are used advantageously to shape

Upper: Dance floor.
Lower: Bar.
Opposite: Counter and soffit of bar.

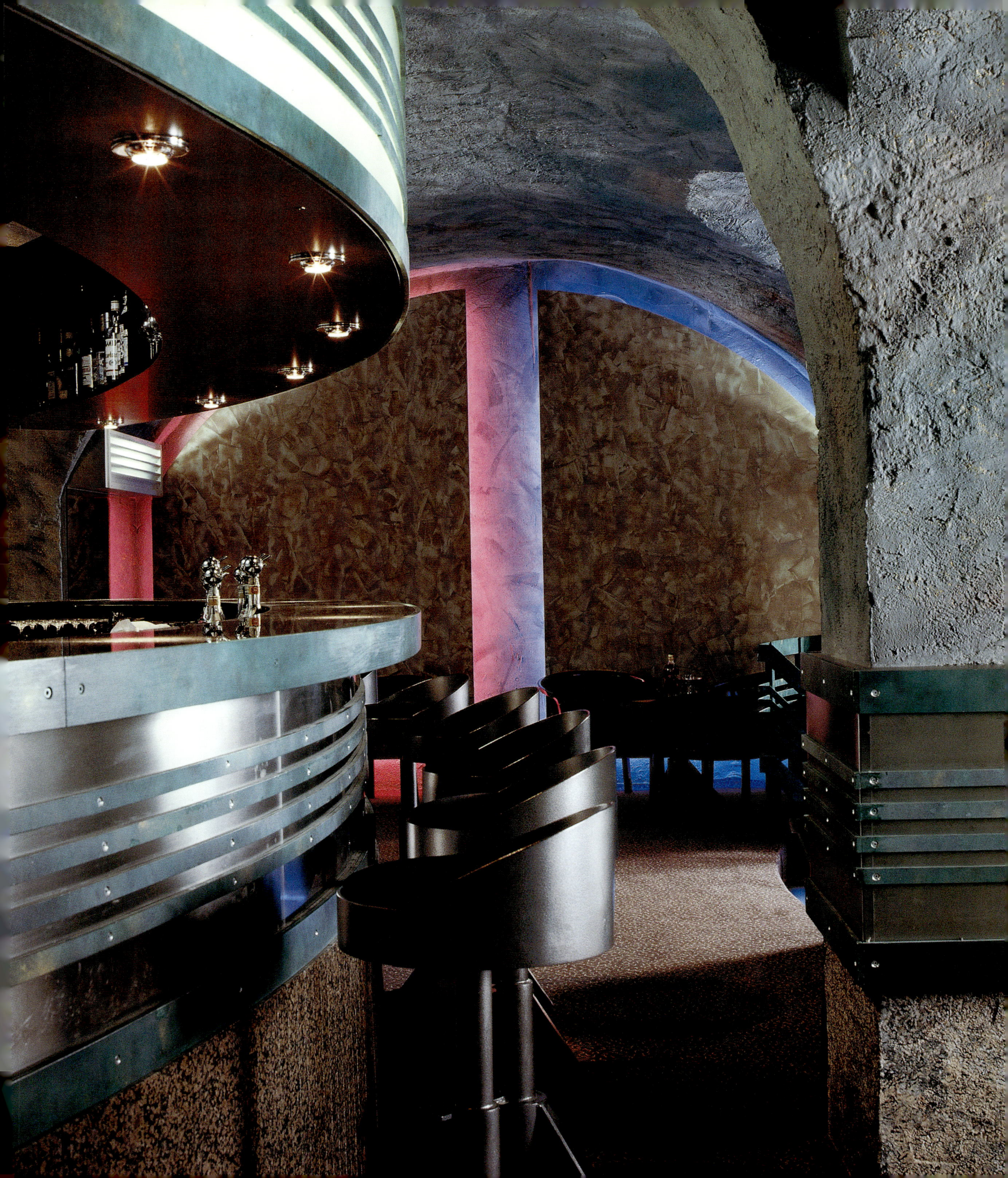

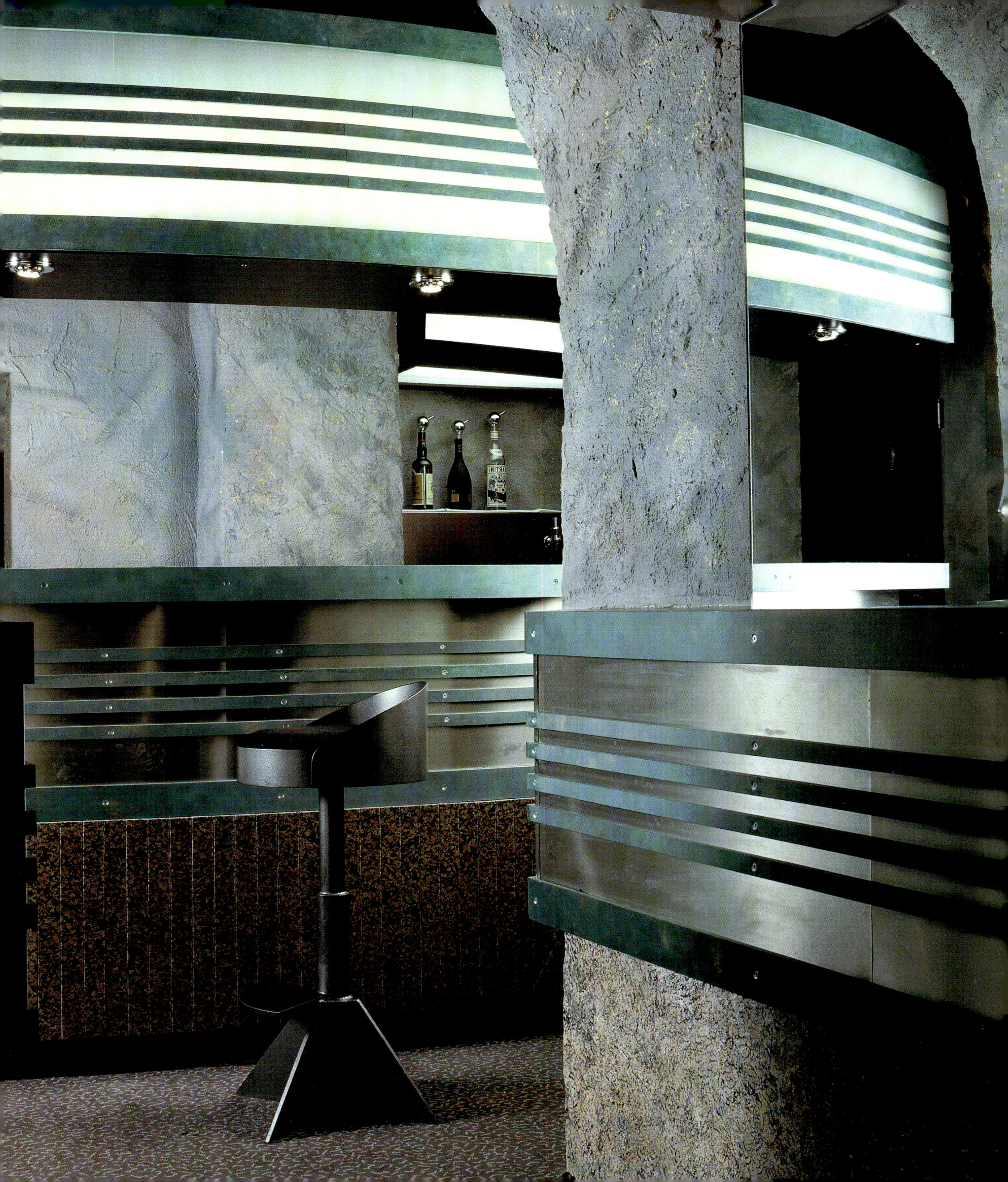

the ambiance of the subterranean interior, including the band of mirror, which exaggerates Chameleon's depth and overall volume, the overhead soffit, which conceals the uplighting and reduces the perceived weight and proximity of the ceiling, and the color scheme, particularly as applied to the walls and ceiling as blues, pinks and golds in a wide, random, brush-stroke pattern, which produces an antique patina. The presence of the band of mirror, stainless steel wainscoting, aluminum light valences and back-illuminated dance floor are reminders that while Chameleon, like Frankfurt itself, harbors fond memories of the past, it can leap into the future at a moment's notice.

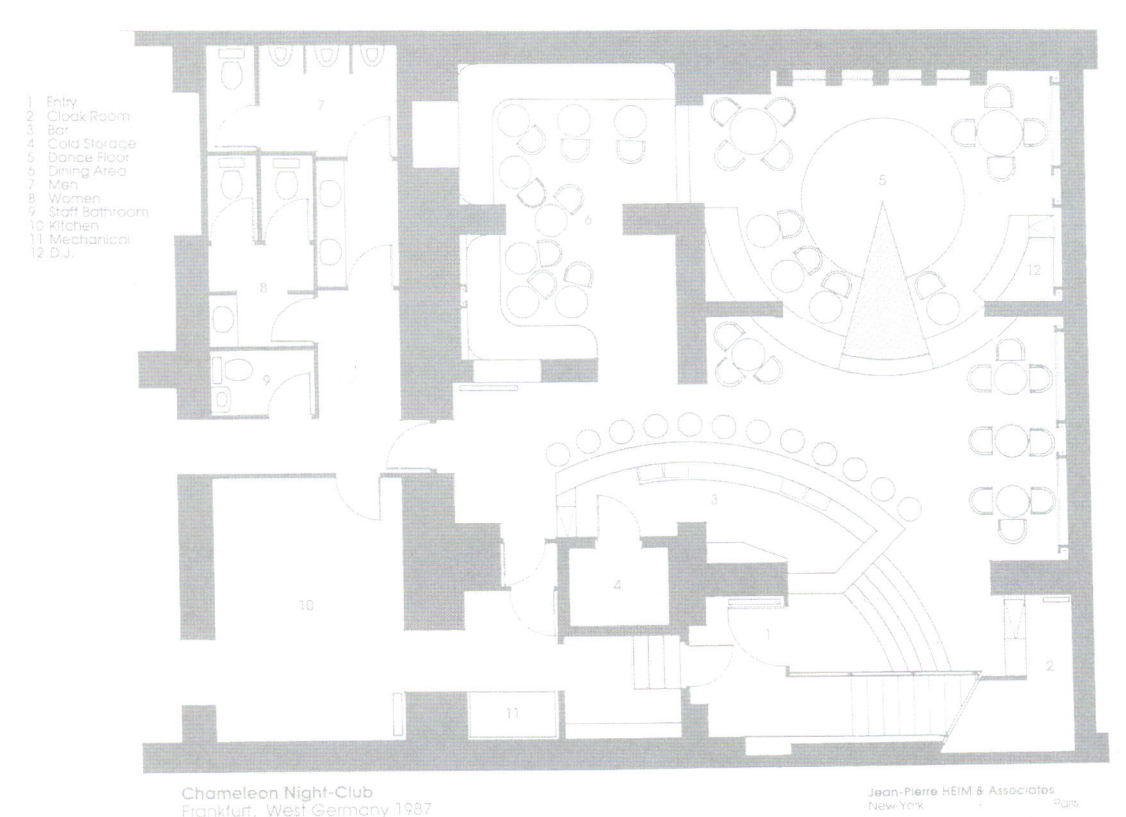

1. Entry
2. Cloak Room
3. Bar
4. Cold Storage
5. Dance Floor
6. Dining Area
7. Men
8. Women
9. Staff Bathroom
10. Kitchen
11. Mechanical
12. D.J.

Chameleon Night-Club
Frankfurt, West Germany 1987

Jean-Pierre HEIM & Associates
New York   Paris

Peace Gardens

Lebanon

A 17-year civil war has not broken the spirit of Lebanon, a nation that has served as an important center of Mediterranean civilization for centuries. Even now, historic sites such as the temples at Baalbek in the northern Bekaa Valley, built by the Romans to honor their deities Jupiter and Bacchus, survive in remarkably good condition, helping to draw tourists back for sightseeing, recreation, cultural activities and culinary arts. To commemorate the reconstruction of the center of Beirut, the capital of Lebanon, Jean-Pierre Heim proposed a series of Peace Gardens for various sites in 1995. The typical construction of the landscape will consist of slabs of stone from Baalbek combined with a cedar tree, the living symbol of Lebanon, and other plantings. Whatever the religious affiliation of the visitor, each Peace Garden will extend a timeless welcome to peace, optimism and renewal.

This page: A scheme with small-scale steps descending to the cedar tree.
Opposite: Benches surrounding the cedar tree represent the essence of this proposal.
Overleaf: Sketches document the impact of the growing cedar tree at a given site.

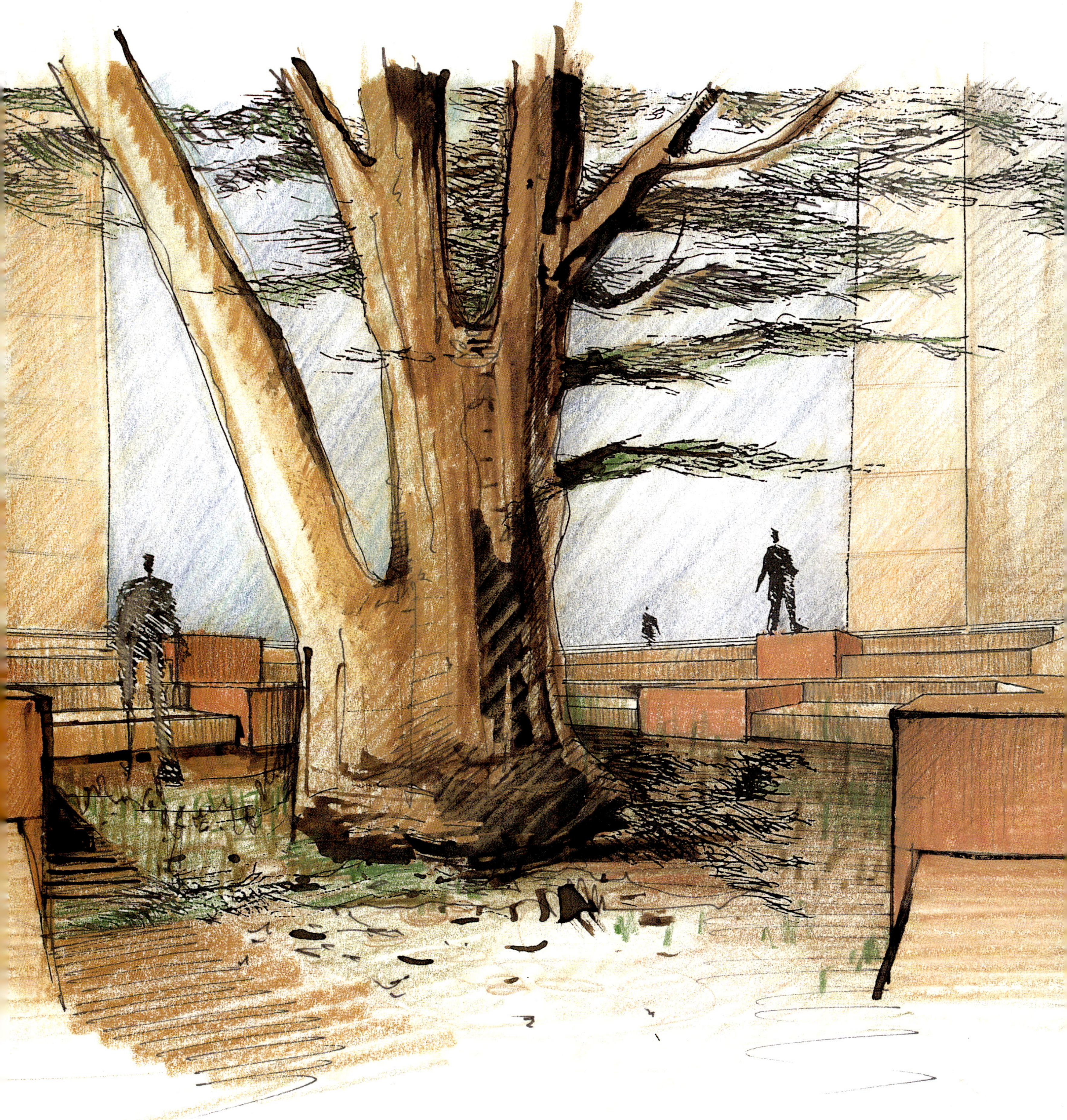

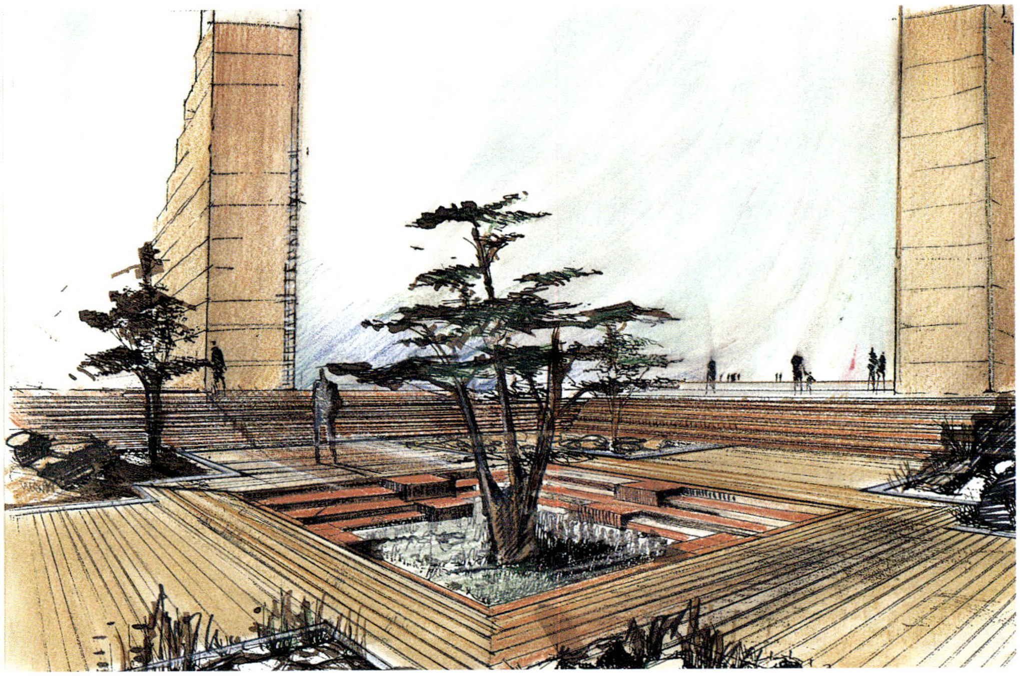

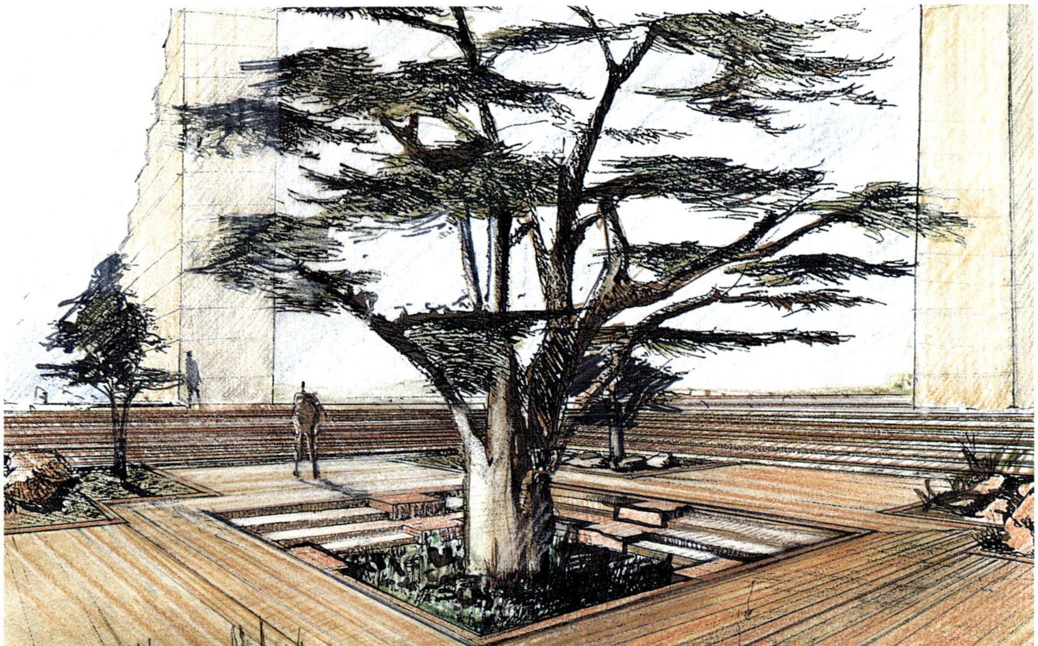

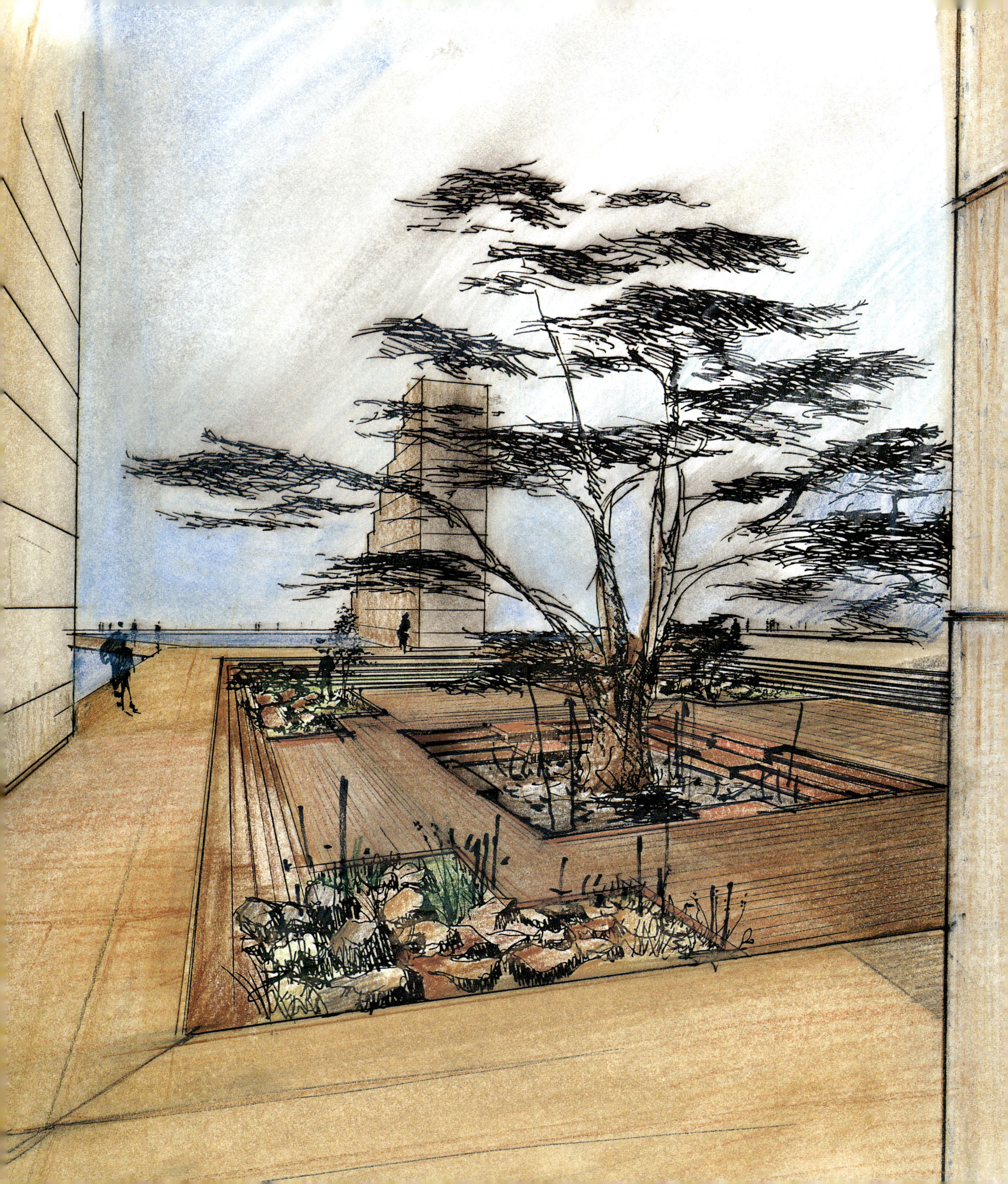

Yasmina Hotel
Morocco, Africa

Everything was close at hand — Berber villages, Roman sites and the Rit Mountains — except the right hotel accommodations for tourists visiting Yasmina, a Moroccan coastal community just 60 kilometers or two and a half hours from Tangier. That explains why Club Med retained Jean-Pierre Heim to renovate two aging hotels from the 1970s and combine them as major components in a new Yasmina Village that would operate 450 guestrooms along with a reception lobby, lounges, three restaurants, a commercial kitchen and redesigned outdoor facilities, including a pool and a theater. One of the existing hotels was a 200-room structure finished in white stucco and tile that clearly acknowledged its northern Moroccan culture and Mediterranean climate. However, the other hotel was a 250-room concrete block structure whose contemporary design had nothing to do with its surroundings. Besides infusing the hotels with a consistent design vision that invoked Orientalism with white stucco walls and yellow and terra cotta accents, tile floors, wood and wrought iron doors, furniture and screens, hand-woven carpets, pottery, lighting fixtures and a decorative motif based on three black circles, Heim created a central village that added a new, 500-seat restaurant and a new landscape design to the remodeled pool and theater. Once the construction team, which made extensive use of local craftsmen and techniques, finished the nine-month project, guests could enter the Club Med grounds and realize they were entering Morocco.

Left: The 700-seat restaurant in the central village.
Above: A typical, wood and wrought iron doorway.
Opposite: A guest bedroom seen through a wrought iron gate.

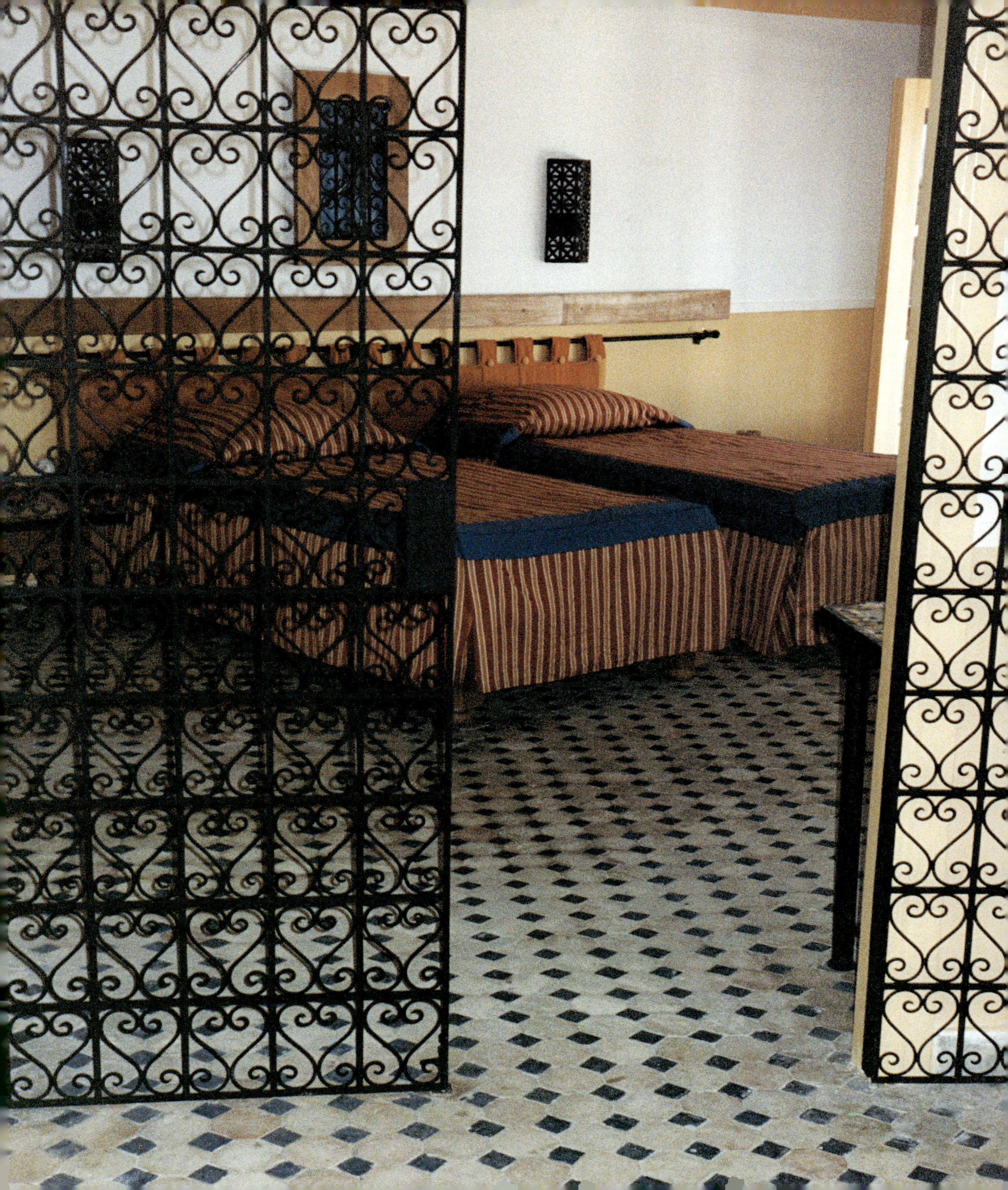

Hotel Le Pavillon Bastille
Paris, France

Nowadays, when eager crowds storm the Bastille area of Paris in the 11th and 12th Arrondissements, they are usually seeking entertainment and shopping rather than revolution. In their pursuit of the Opéra Bastille, the nightclubs that crowd the nearby rue de Lappe and the chic shops lining the Rue de la Roquette, discerning people have looked across the street from the Opéra and fallen in love with Le Pavillon Bastille. This new, 25-room hotel (including one suite) at 65 Rue de Lyon, described by Frommer's as "a bold, innovative hotel in a town house" and characterized by Fodor's as "a smart address for savvy travelers who appreciate getting perks for less," has been designed by Jean-Pierre Heim to be quite unlike any other in the City of Light. Its 19th-century structure, which was previously operated as a transient residence for government employees and visiting guests, has been refurbished as an intimate, high-style lodging with a contemporary interior design that playfully acknowledges its surroundings — especially the musical world just steps from its door. For the hip, devoted clientele who apparently regard the hotel as their own, well-kept secret, the aura is present from the time they enter the courtyard, with its 17th-century fountain and black, wrought iron cafe chairs and tables, and ascend a short flight of steps beneath a blue and yellow canopy — everything inside follows a blue-and-yellow color palette — to the reception lobby. The reception lobby lounge appropriately sets the stage for the gue-

This page: Lobby lounge appointed in the hotel's signature blue and yellow color palette.
Opposite: Wall panels and doors in the lobby bear the five-line pattern of musical notation.

strooms, bar and breakfast room to follow with a smartly tailored interior of sensuously curving chairs and sofas upholstered in yellow and blue leather atop a glistening checkerboard floor of black granite and beige Capri stone or a lush checkerboard carpet of black and blue squares, surrounded by mottled yellow walls and topped by a sleek, mirrored ceiling that reflects the highlights of the glass-topped cocktail tables and bright chrome torchieres below. Like much else in the hotel, these distinctive furnishings represent mainly the designs of Jean-Pierre Heim, and are produced by his furniture company, Design Connection International. While the guestrooms are relatively small, the interior design arranges the space to

This page: Typical guestroom makes effective use of small area with compact furnishings and mirrored wall.
Opposite: Guestroom sitting area and desk (above) and details of the lobby's typical chair and cocktail table.

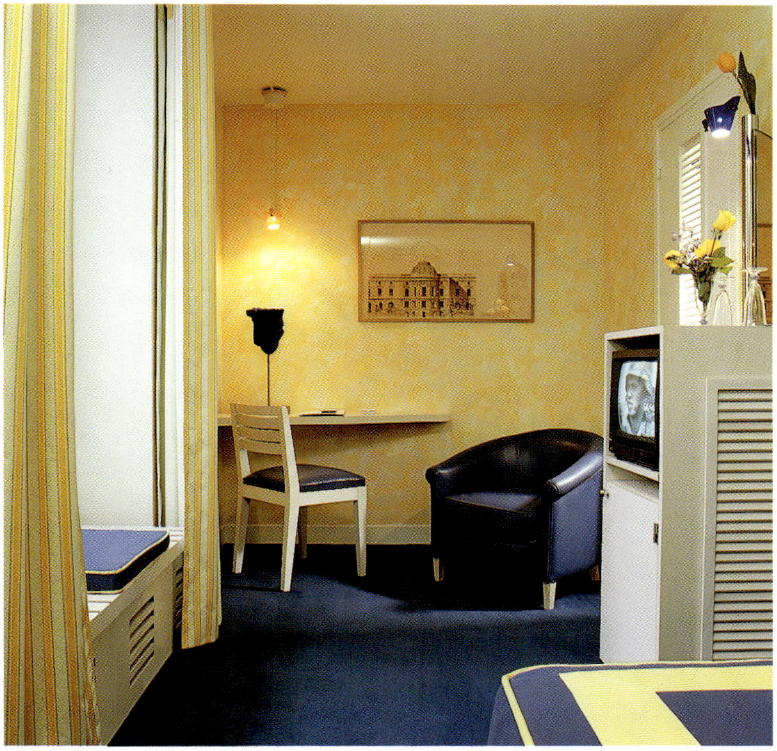

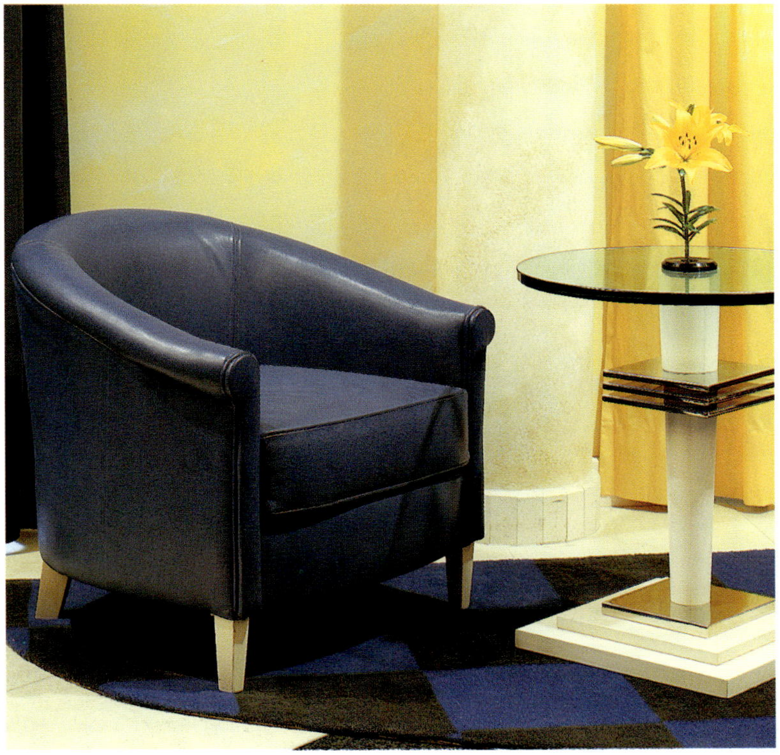

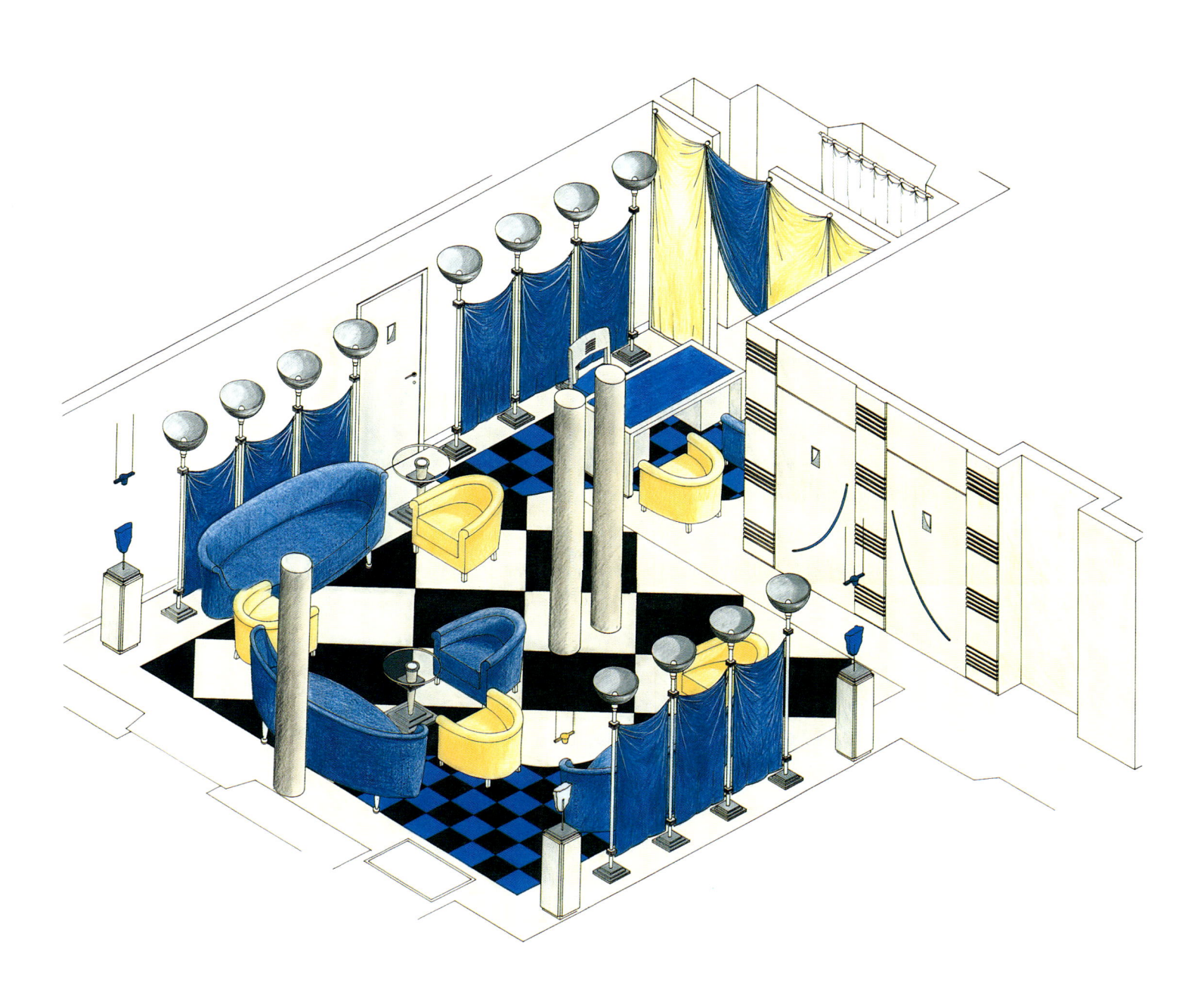

This page: The lobby lounge floor plan plays orthogonal geometry against curvilinear furnishings.
Opposite: Le Orchestra, the hotel breakfast room, animates a cellar space with lighting and color.

advantage by incorporating such compact furnishings as the storage unit for the mini-bar and TV, a custom-designed cabinet with a curved mirror and built-in cylindrical vase, and visual devices like the mirrored wall above the headboard. (The handsome architectural prints on the walls are flea market finds, adding an idiosyncratic touch that is a trademark of the architect.) As for food service at the hotel, the existing, vaulted cellar has been transformed into Le Orchestra, a 25-seat breakfast room furnished with bleached oak chairs and paneling, blue and yellow upholstery, blue carpet and handpainted blue walls.

Clearly, every detail helps tell the story of Le Pavillon Bastille. You don't have to be a music lover to appreciate that Jean-Pierre Heim has planted musical motifs throughout the hotel, in the rugs that echo the contours of grand pianos, door knobs that resemble flutes, wall panels carrying the five-line pattern of musical notation, and more. Once you step out to explore the neighborhood, a block south of Place de la Bastille and close to the Marais district, Place des Vosges, and the avant-garde art scene along the Île Saint-Louis, the hotel's harmonious environment will have prepared you to expect music everywhere you go.

le pavillon
BASTILLE

79

Abajour

New York, New York USA

Restaurateur Anatole Iwanezuk, owner of Abajour: An American Bistro, knew something radical was needed when he bought the 110-seat, two-level restaurant called Tony McGregor on Manhattan's Upper East Side. The image of the existing restaurant was that of a pub, dark, club-like and complete with green walls and mahogany woodwork. Determined that the public see his business as a restaurant rather than a bar, Iwanezuk retained Jean-Pierre Heim to design a completely new environment in 2000. The architect's successful solution reverses the lighting level with a seemingly weightless space built around the concept of a lampshade — "abatjour" means "lampshade" in French, a word that Iwanezuk simplified for marketing purposes — and flooded with direct and filtered light. Consequently, the interior is adorned with off-white and sheer lampshades everywhere the eye can see, mounted on table lamps atop the bar, hovering like attentive wait staff on floor lamps beside the tables in the dining rooms, and suspended from the ceiling above the entry to the main dining room as a cluster of nine lampshades sheltered within a larger one. Yet numerous other means are employed to convince guests they are relaxing in the shade at a sun-splashed resort, including back-lighted wood Venetian blinds that help divide the dining rooms into smaller areas, sunny yellow paint on the walls, pale yellow clapboard siding around the bar, white slipcovers on all seating, from the bar stools and dining chairs on the main floor to the sofas in the upstairs lounge, and an 18-foot-high white curtain panel draped across the two-story-high glass storefront. The consequences have been no less bright. The New York Times hailed Abajour as "Just what the neighborhood needs: a respectable neighborhood bistro with pleasing decor, an attractive menu and some well-priced wines." Not only do people look wonderful basking in the flattering glow of Abajour, so does the acclaimed menu from executive chef David Kenuul.

Upper: Exterior at 1134 First Avenue.
Lower: Lampshades light the bar and main dining room.
Opposite: A view of the bar and two-story storefront.

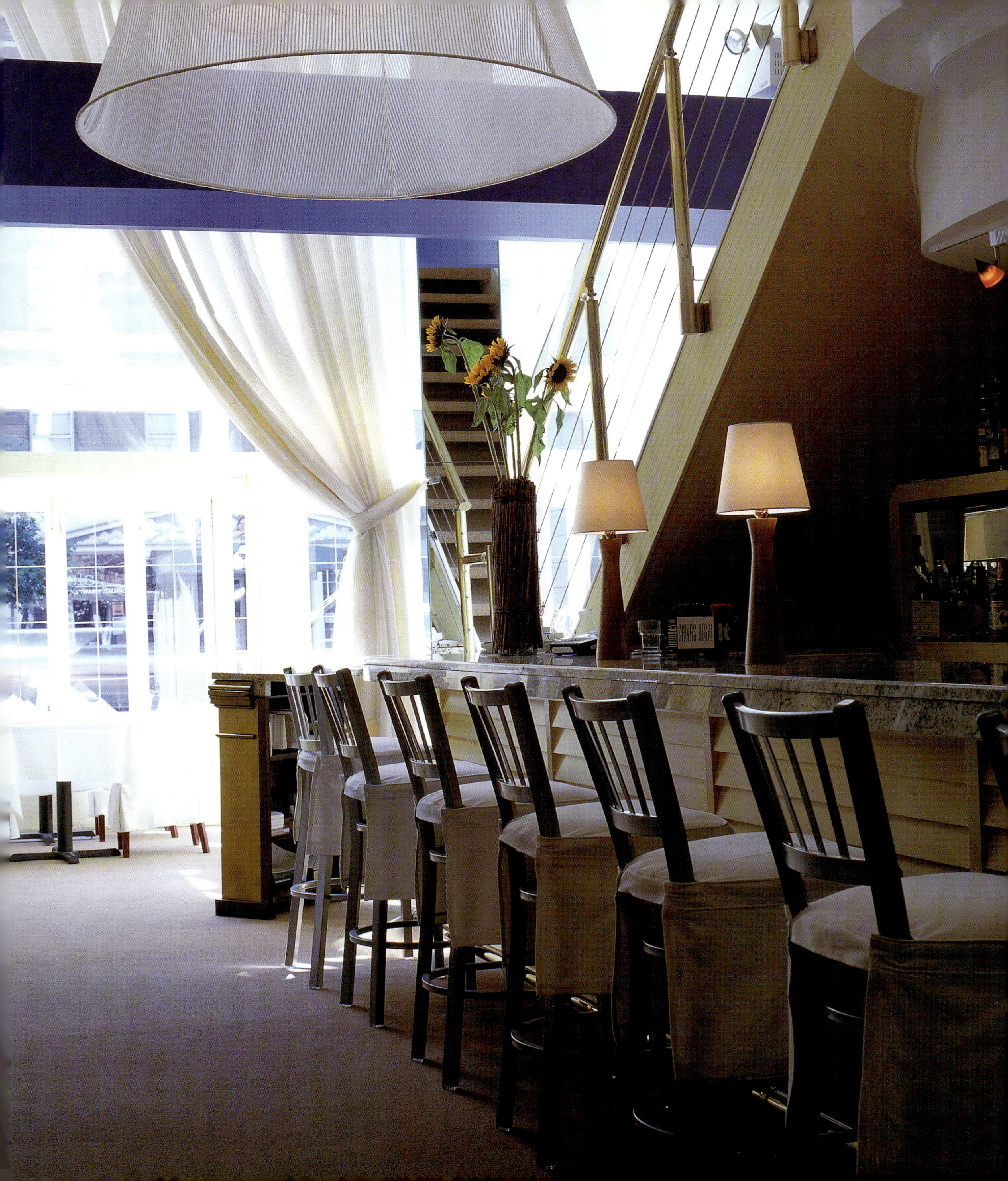

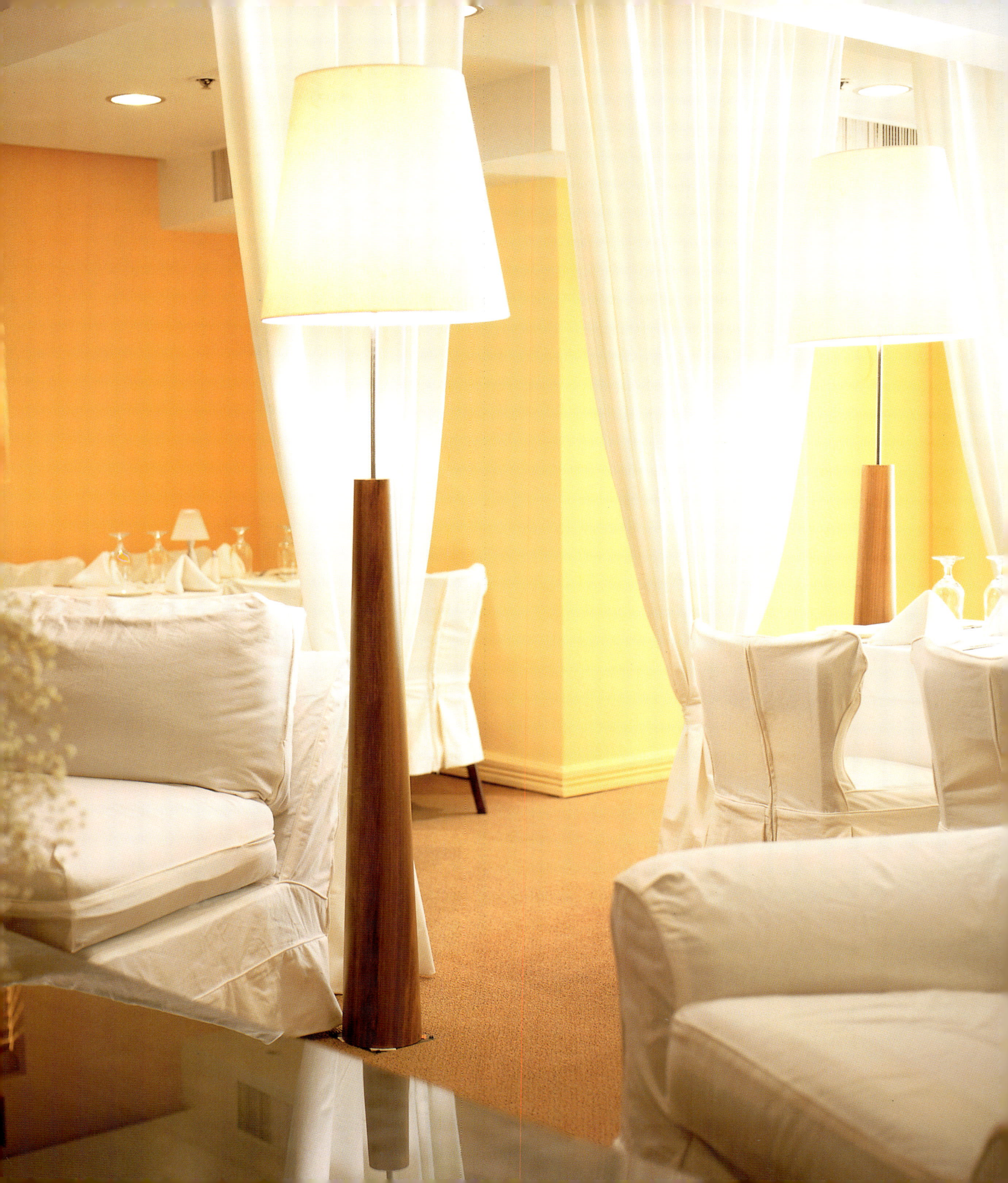

Upper: Floor lamps are supplemented by back-lighted Venetian blinds.
Lower: A cluster of nine lampshades sheltered within a larger one.
Opposite: The upstairs lounge and dining room.

Ichthys
Paris, France

Who would think fish could influence French fashion? Think again. Ichthys is a three-story, 2,500-square-foot prototype fashion boutique where fish abound, within a Beaux Arts building on the chic rue Francois Premier in Paris. This high-end store for men and women has been designed by Jean-Pierre Heim and Galal Mahmoud to create effective selling space inspired by the fact that "ichthys" means "fish" in Greek. Interestingly, the architects have exploited the symmetry of fish to shape the boutique's logo, floor plan and interior details without distorting the Beaux Arts building's long, narrow floors. Fish shapes combine with handsome, conventional store fixtures wherever customers look, such as a stainless steel replica of the logo set into the bleached oak floor at the entrance, an inlaid limestone oval at the center of the floor, and an oval opening in the ceiling that transforms the second story into a mezzanine balcony. Since the design is spreading to stores in Monte Carlo, Nice, Osaka and Tokyo, affluent shoppers worldwide may soon find themselves fishing for fashion too.

Upper: The mezzanine's blue light and stainless steel balustrade strongly evoke a boat at sea.
Lower: The ground floor is furnished with gray furniture and a rounded display case for men's ties.
Opposite: The view from the mezzanine looking down through a fish-shaped opening to the ground floor.

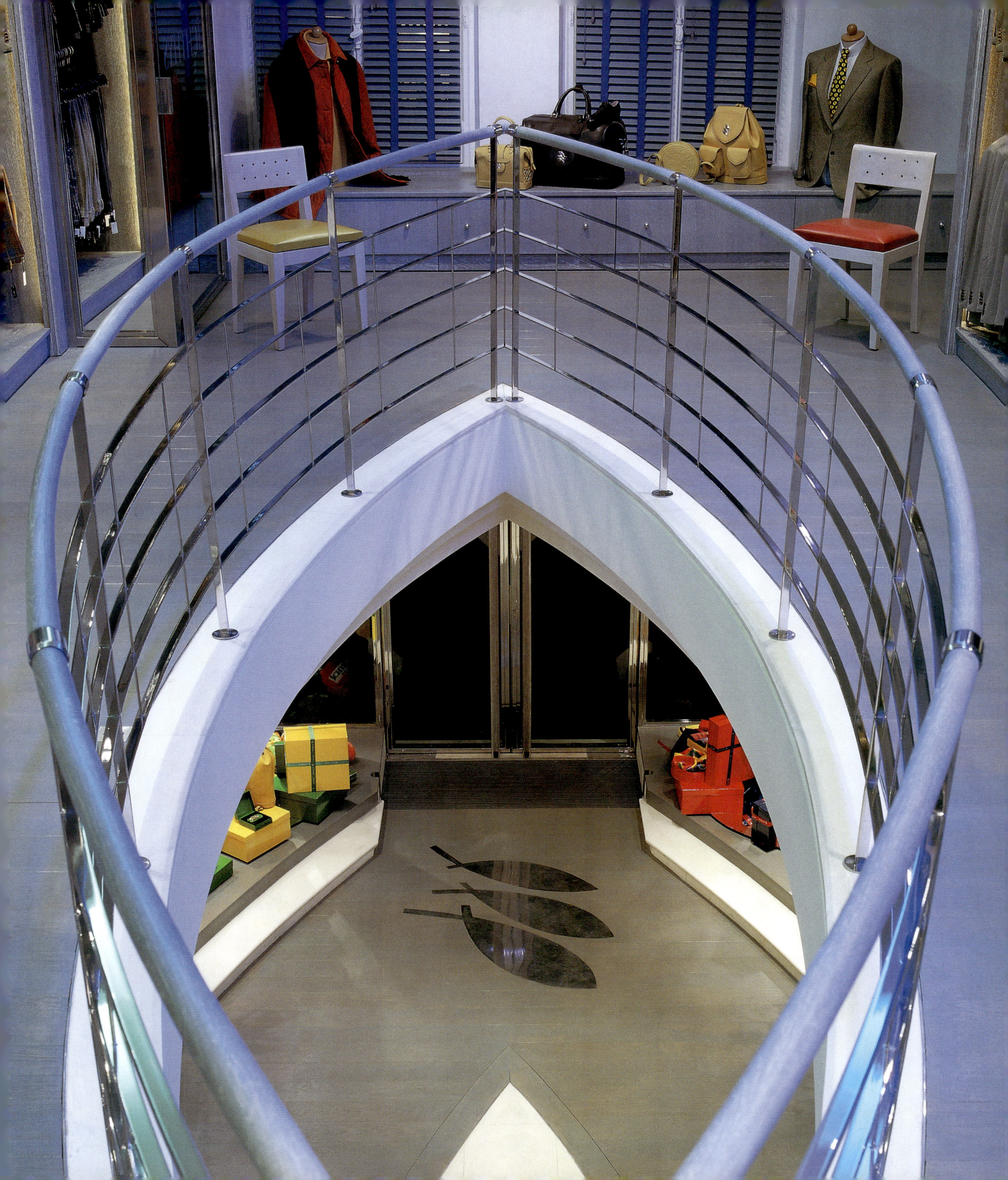

Puiforcat

Paris, France

If customers shopping for silver tableware and hollowware and fine china at the meticulously tailored Puiforcat store in Paris prior to the company's recent change of ownership were to sense the gentle sway of an ocean liner at sea, they would probably not have been disturbed. The 7,000-square-foot, two-story retail space, located on the avenue Matignon in an historic district just off the Champs-Élysées, was commissioned in 1989 from Jean-Pierre Heim by Eliane Scali, then president of Puiforcat, as part of a redesign of the company's worldwide image that also took Heim to Monaco, New York and Tokyo. The project quickly became a homage to the achievements of Jean Puiforcat, one of France's greatest silversmiths, whose family founded the company in 1820. Since one of Puiforcat's most memorable triumphs was the Art Deco silverware he created for the legendary passenger ship Normandie, launched in 1935 with ornamentation by Lalique, and the store's floor plan was triangular in form, much like a ship's prow, Heim transformed the former home of a famed nightclub into a space reminiscent of a luxury liner. One could easily imagine Puiforcat beaming with pride at the results. The design of the store, which was approximately 10-feet wide at the entrance and 70-feet wide at the broadest point, acknowledged

This page: Evening at the entrance to the store.
Opposite: Stair finials reproduce sculptures by Jean Puiforcat.
Following pages: The center of the upper level selling floor ;
Upper level views of the staircase.
Overleaf: A rendering of the new storefront.

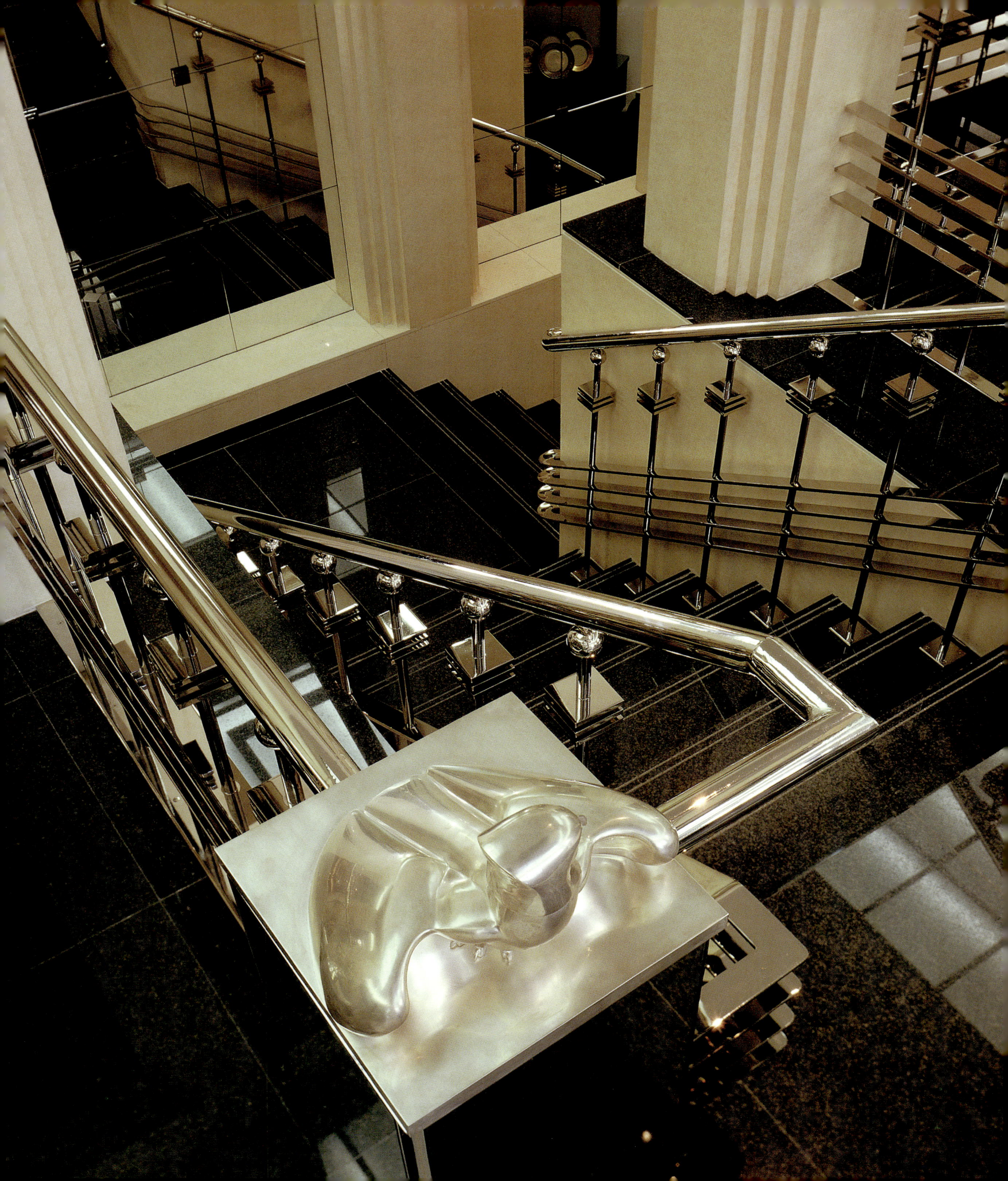

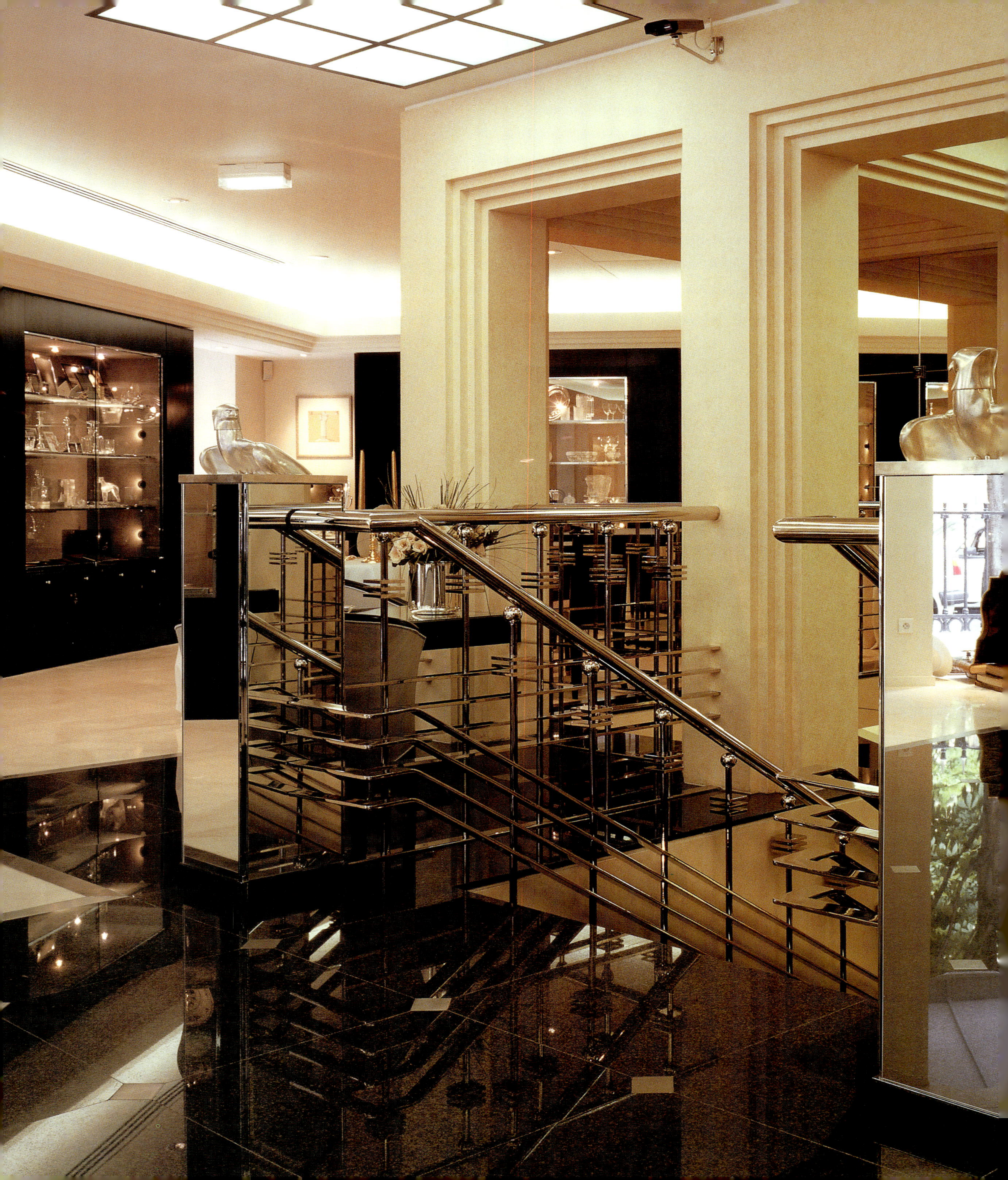

Puiforcat's signature style by means of a glamorous interior of glistening black granite, beige marble, stainless steel and mirrors that was furnished with custom furniture designed by Heim in the Art Deco style. At its center, the staircase, highlighted by jewel-like railings and topped with silver reproductions of sculptures by Puiforcat as finials, acted as a brilliant beacon that all but guaranteed that customers visited the product displays on the upper level of the store. Of course, there was little likelihood that customers would fail to notice anything in an environment that could easily have sailed aboard the Normandie.

PUIFOR

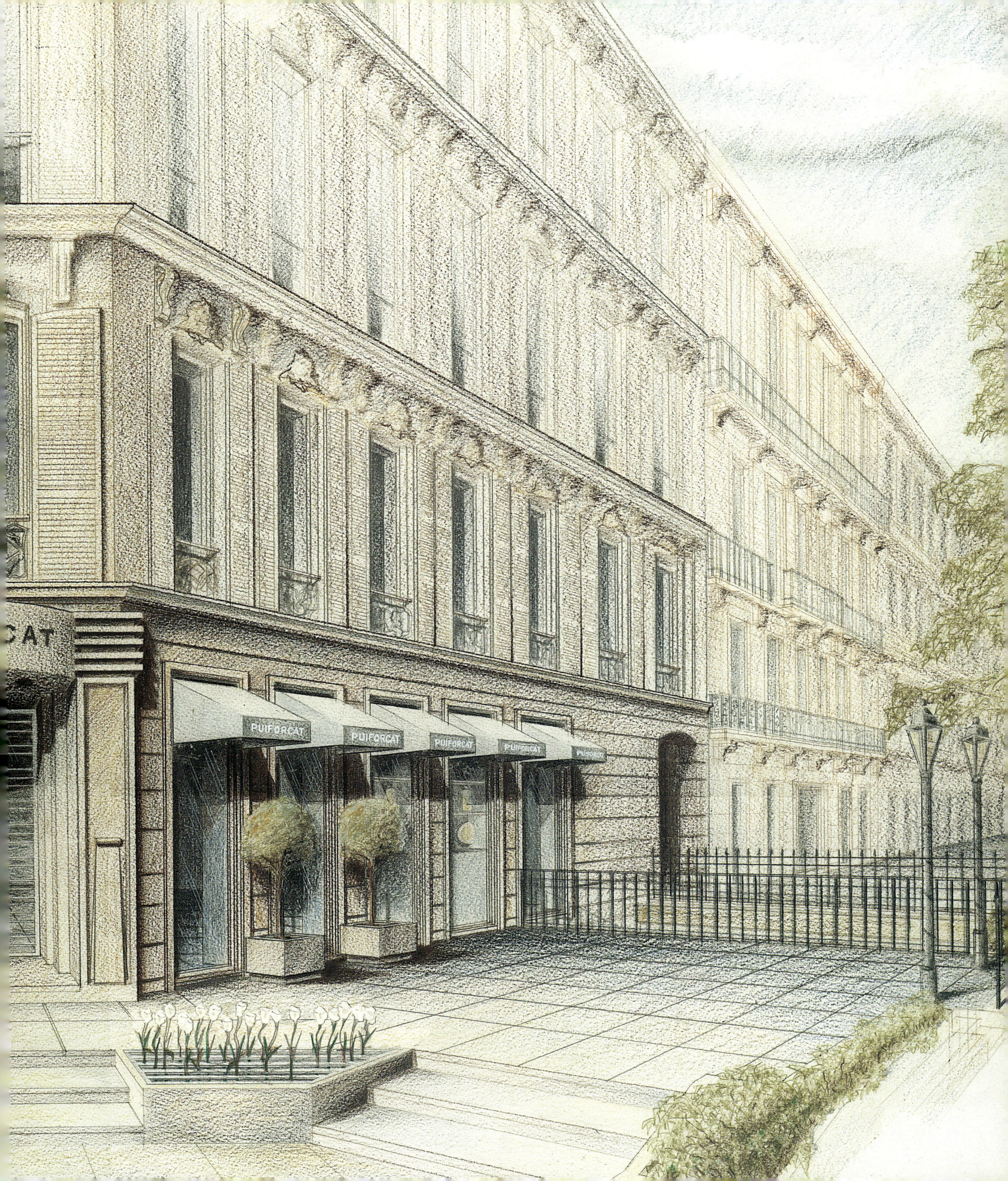
CAT
PUIFORCAT
PUIFORCAT
PUIFORCAT
PUIFORCAT
PUIFORCAT

Christian Lacroix
Paris, France

Born in 1951 in Arles, in the south of France, in 1951, Christian Lacroix has taken the Mediterranean sun wherever he has gone during a dazzling career in haute couture. His distinctive look blends playfulness and style through a bright color palette, "neo-Baroque" style, characterized by the "pouf" ball gown he reintroduced in the 1980s, and such eclectic combinations as modernity and tradition, technology and heritage, and Western civilization and non-Western cultures in his couture, jewelry and costumes for theater and opera. For the new Paris flagship store of his fashion house, Lacroix asked Jean-Pierre Heim and architect Remy de Bourbon Parme to capture the atmosphere and colors that infuse the seaside towns of southern France and Italy. In an added twist to the design brief, the couturier also wanted to acknowledge the graceful architecture of the 1930s building on the Avenue Montaigne, distinguished by its undulating facades, that houses the retail store. Heim's spirited solution adheres faithfully to Lacroix's wishes. From the Mediterranean garden planted with flowers in shades of yellow, the couturier's favorite color, to a bowed storefront and such curvilinear interior elements as a curving soffit, bearing a painted frieze from Lacroix's C'est la Vie perfume, below a sky blue ceiling cove and a billowing stone wall that ends beside a weathered stone portico now converted into a vitrine, the design of the store is an architectural celebration of the Lacroix brand. Even the store's whimsical furniture, designed by Garouste and Bonetti, contributes to the

This page: Ceiling cove in the color of the Mediterranean sky. Opposite: Bowed storefront with Venetian posts and Mediterranean garden.

CHRISTIAN LACROIX

Upper: Christian Lacroix's initials as a store motif.
Lower: Main selling space with curving soffit and wall.
Opposite: Old stone portico converted into a vitrine.

mood. If customers need any further reminders that they are visiting the House of Lacroix — not that they do — there are Mediterranean palm and cypress trees, both rare in Paris, and a pair of Venetian posts in red and gold, Lacroix's other favored colors, guarding the entrance to this appealing morsel of the Côte d'Azur in Paris.

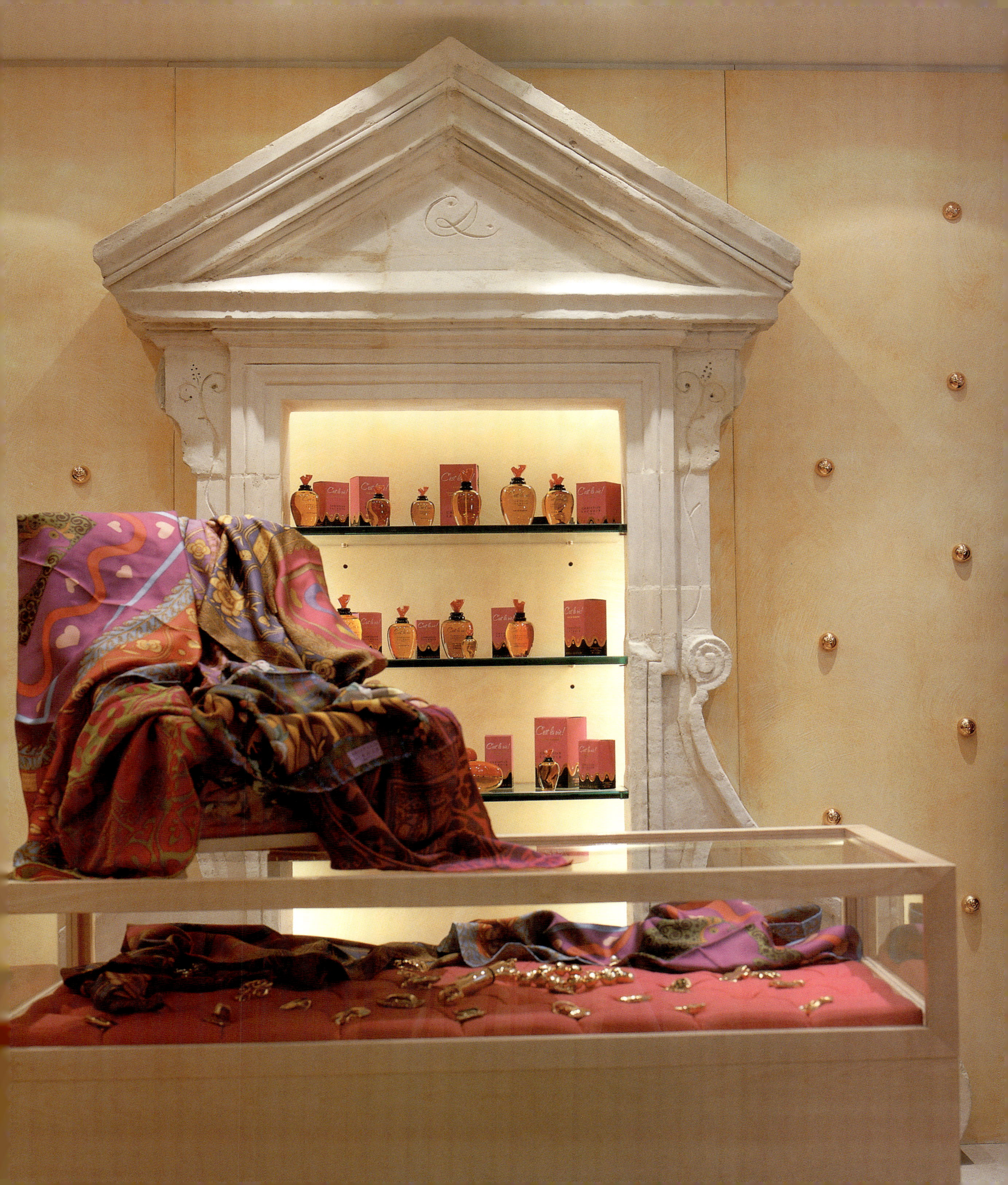
C'est la vie!

Revillon
New York, New York USA

Upper: Design sketch.
Lower: Display fixtures and vitrines.
Opposite: Haute couture boutique.

When you have been a storied furrier and purveyor of luxury items for over 275 years, as is the legacy of Paris-based Revillon, your U.S. boutiques must be opulent in a signature style that is recognizable wherever your customers are. The Revillon flagship store in New York was designed by Jean-Pierre Heim in 1997 to provide just such a distinctive milieu. In the majestic, 3,800-square-foot facility at 717 Fifth Avenue, Heim has skillfully exploited the long, narrow footprint of the space to stage a dramatic procession through a series of bays defined by curved walls. Outside, the public views a spectacular, 100-foot-long, wraparound array of window displays staged in front of the concave sides of individual bays, with a large decorative metal screen providing a frame for the bays and doubling as a security gate. Inside, customers proceed from bay to bay to view every category of merchandise, ranging from gift accessories to haute couture, in a path that culminates in the haute couture boutique, resplendent under a gilded

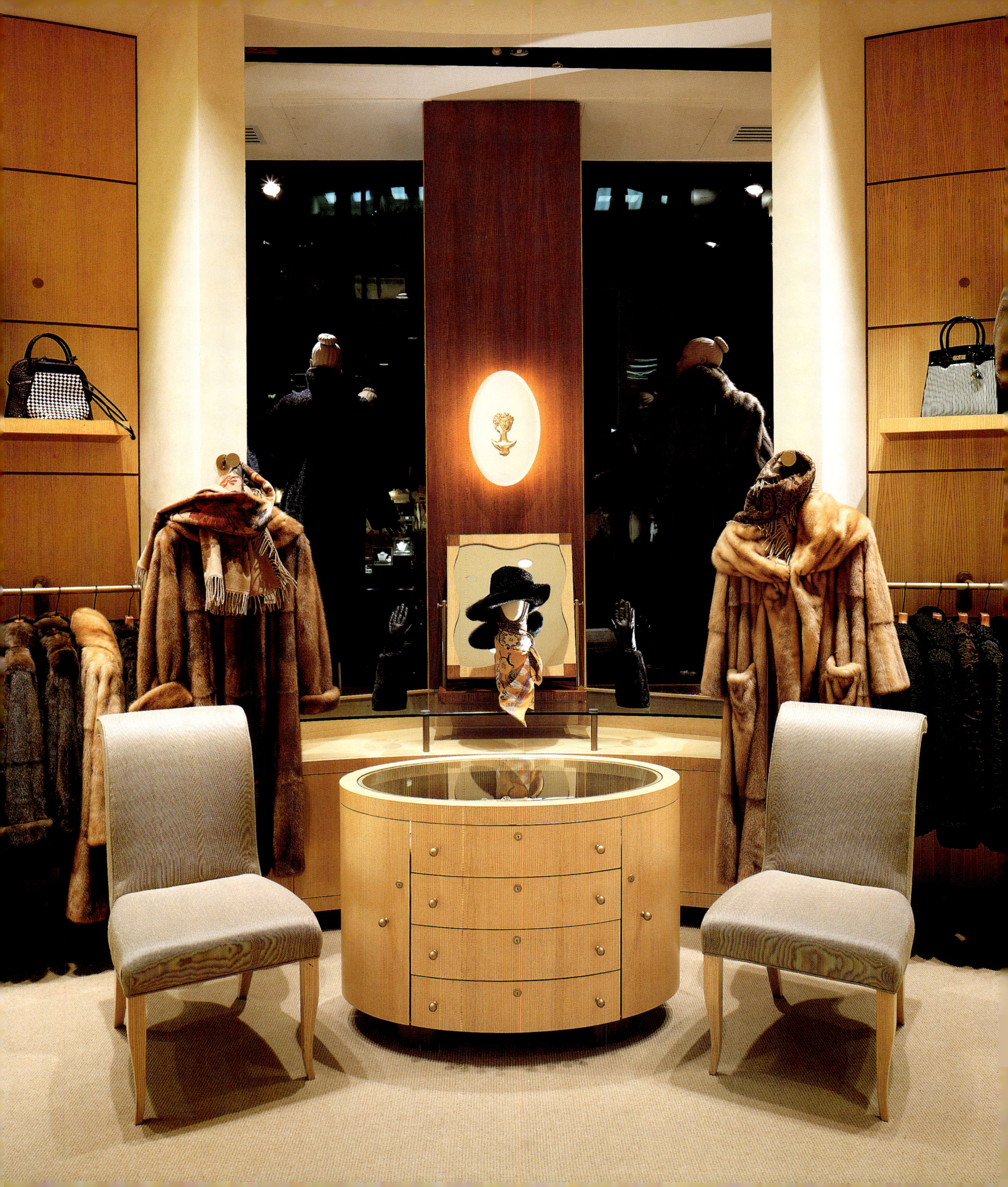

dome set into a 24-foot-high ceiling. Furnishings complement the space without upstaging the merchandise, combining cherry and ash inlaid cabinetry, generous armchairs, curved banquettes, stone accents, carpet and a rich array of lighting to squire Revillon's furs, outerwear, rainwear, ready to wear and accessories to market. The new retail store proudly reasserts Revillon's century-long presence on Fifth Avenue, serving a clientele that Rebecca De Vives, former president of Revillon, described as "customers who want European quality and design and believe in buying established luxury brands."

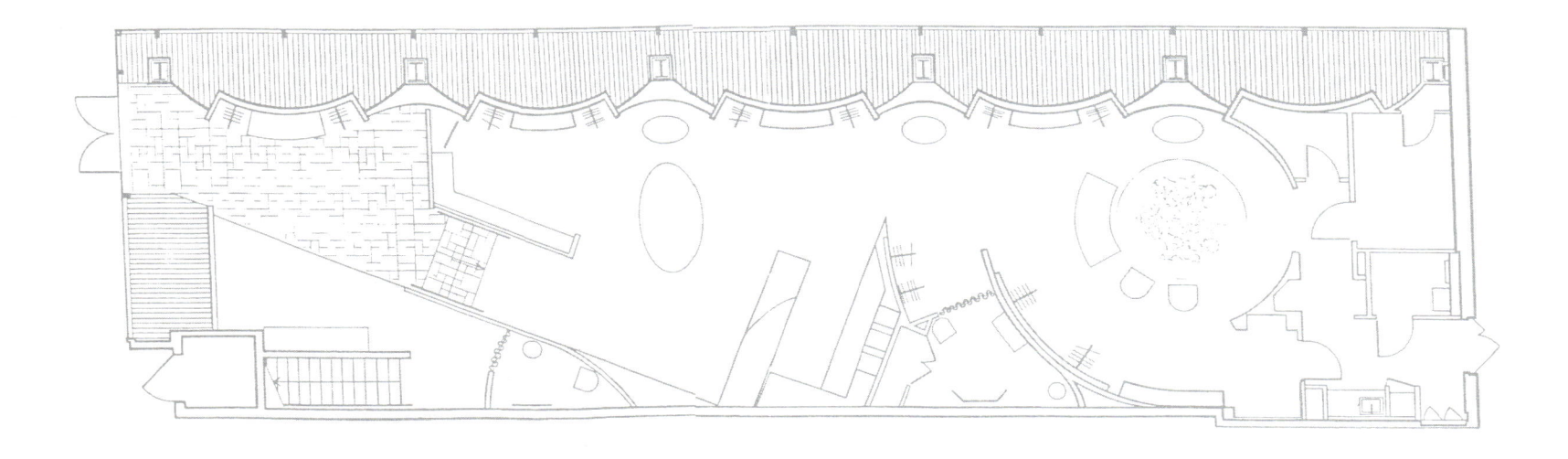

This page: Dressing room.
Opposite: Fur salon.

Baccarat
New York, New York USA

To be young, hip and living the Baccarat lifestyle! Affluent, young trendsetters on New York's Madison Avenue may not realize the House of Baccarat traces its origin to 1764, the year France's King Louis XV gave Bishop Montmorency-Laval of Metz permission to found a glassworks in the village of Baccarat in Lorraine. Indeed, the purveyor of fine crystal, tabletop, vases, decorative accessories, lighting and jewelry, active in New York since 1948, launched a marketing campaign to shift its consumer image from tabletop to lifestyle, targeting a youthful audience. Of course, Baccarat has no intention of ignoring established clientele. Accordingly, the retail store at 625 Madison Avenue, designed by Jean-Pierre Heim in 1996, provides a showcase for Baccarat to draw customers of all ages. The 5,000-square foot, two-story boutique reaches out to pedestrians with its 30-foot by 90-foot glass facade and four display windows, offering tantalizing glimpses of its products that are hard to resist. Once customers have stepped inside and onto the plush carpet, dyed in the classic Baccarat red, they are surrounded by a cool, crisp environment that straddles modernity and tradition with uncommon ease. The store's modern interiors are open spaces finished in light sycamore walls and divided into numerous enclaves by display cases, vitrines and other store fixtures of wood and glass. Consequently, Baccarat's products use the environment as a foil for their modern and classic designs, letting more decorative pieces such as its magnificent chandeliers remind customers that the company was young more than two centuries ago — and still is.

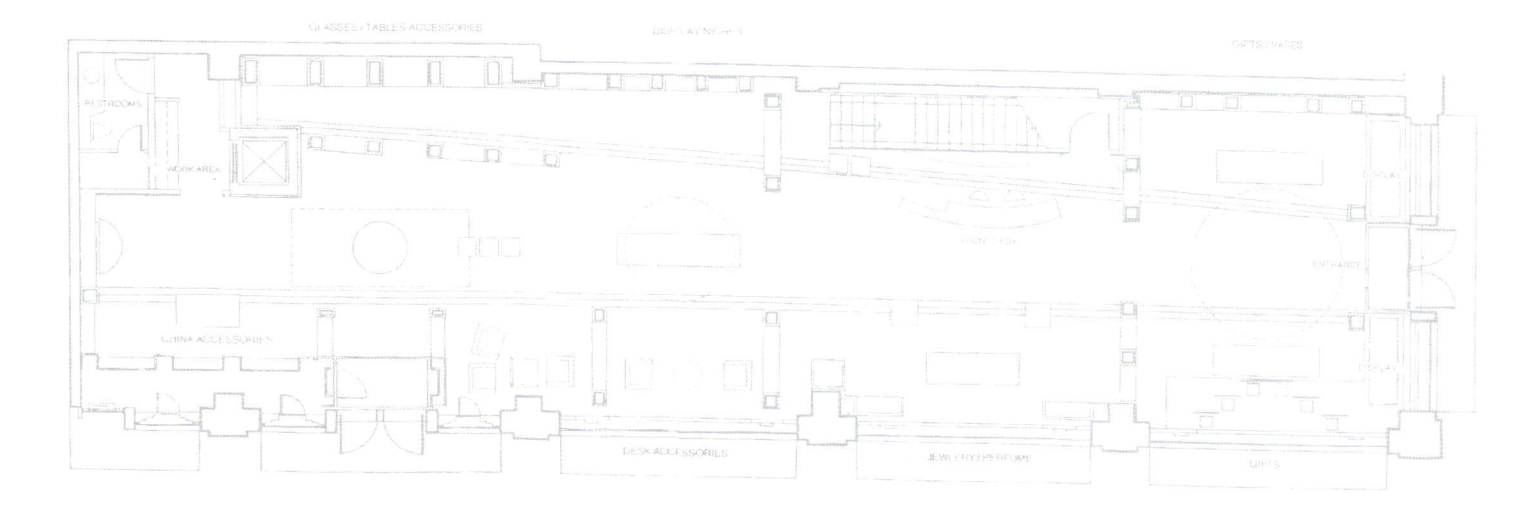

Upper: Design concept for display fixtures.
Lower: Floor plan with extensive glass facade.
Opposite: Perspective along main store axis.

Nicolas Feuillatte

Paris, France

Connoisseurs of the finest Champagnes cherish Champagne Nicolas Feuillatte. One of the world's leading brands, it is the creation of a unique association of 4,500 growers grouped into 85 cooperatives. These growers, controlling nearly 2,200 hectares of land, supply grapes from all the vineyards of the appellation (Montagne de Reims, Côte des Blancs, Vallée de la Marne, Sézannais and Côte des Bar) to be transformed by the Cellar Master into Champagne Nicolas Feuillatte.

cashwrap counter on the first floor and a tasting room and office in the basement, celebrates the making and enjoyment of Champagne. The ground floor is traditional in character, using such warm materials as stucco plaster walls, exotic Iroko woodwork and brass hardware and accents, all illuminated by recessed spot lights under a flat ceiling with a curving soffit, to invite customers inside. By contrast, the basement is cool and modern, evoking a wine cellar by

To present Champagne Nicolas Feuillatte properly to customers on the prestigious Rue du Faubourg St. Honoré in Paris, Jean-Pierre Heim has designed a retail store that symbolizes refined luxury and simplicity. Everything in the two-story space, including retail display fixtures and a

employing a vaulted ceiling of perforated aluminum, indirect blue lighting, wood storage bins, sandblasted glass, and wood plank flooring with inlaid trenches of black and white stones. It's an invitation to visit Champagne Nicolas Feuillatte that Parisians are likely to accept again and again.

This page: Retail display on first floor.
Opposite: Stairs to basement tasting room.

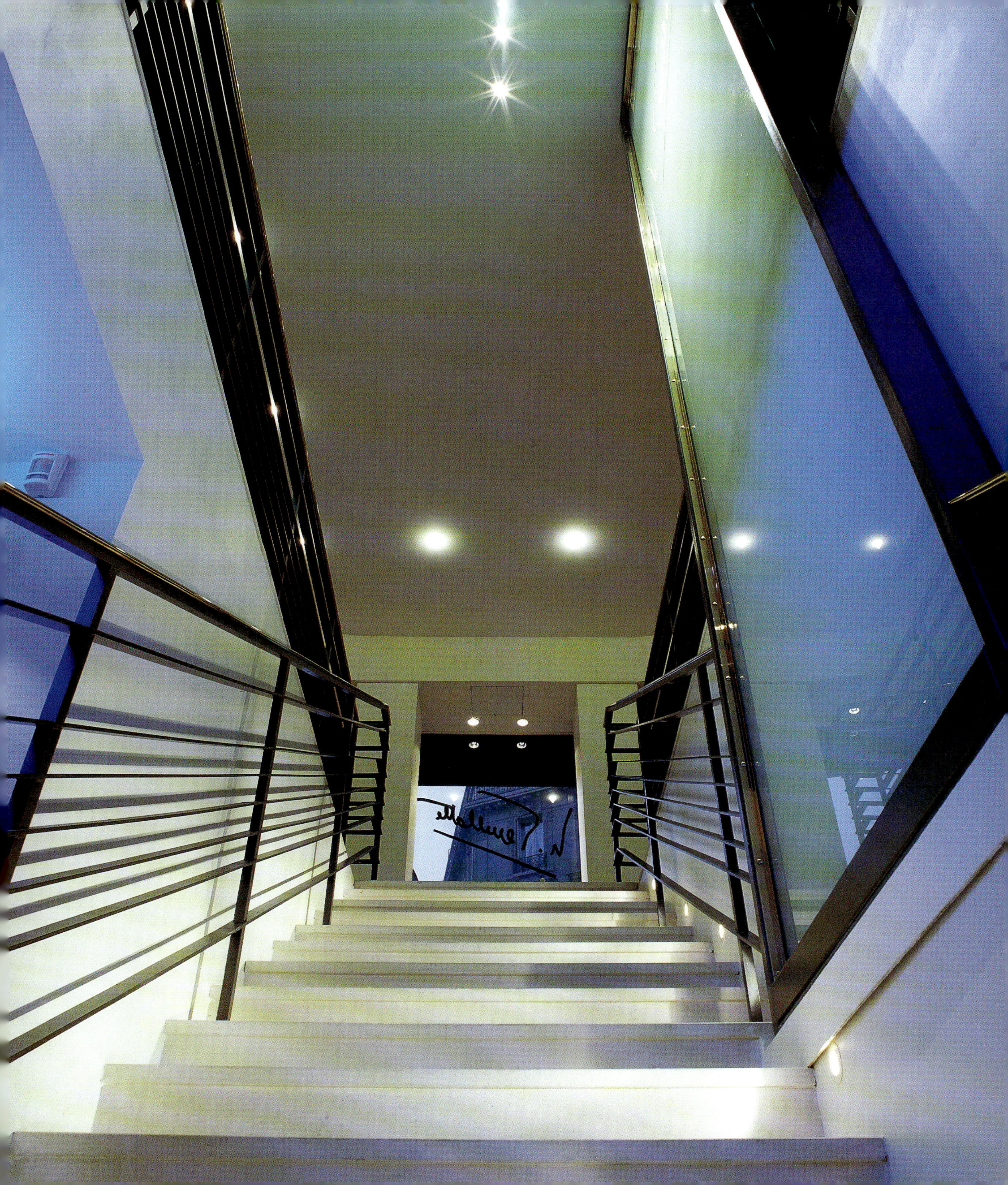

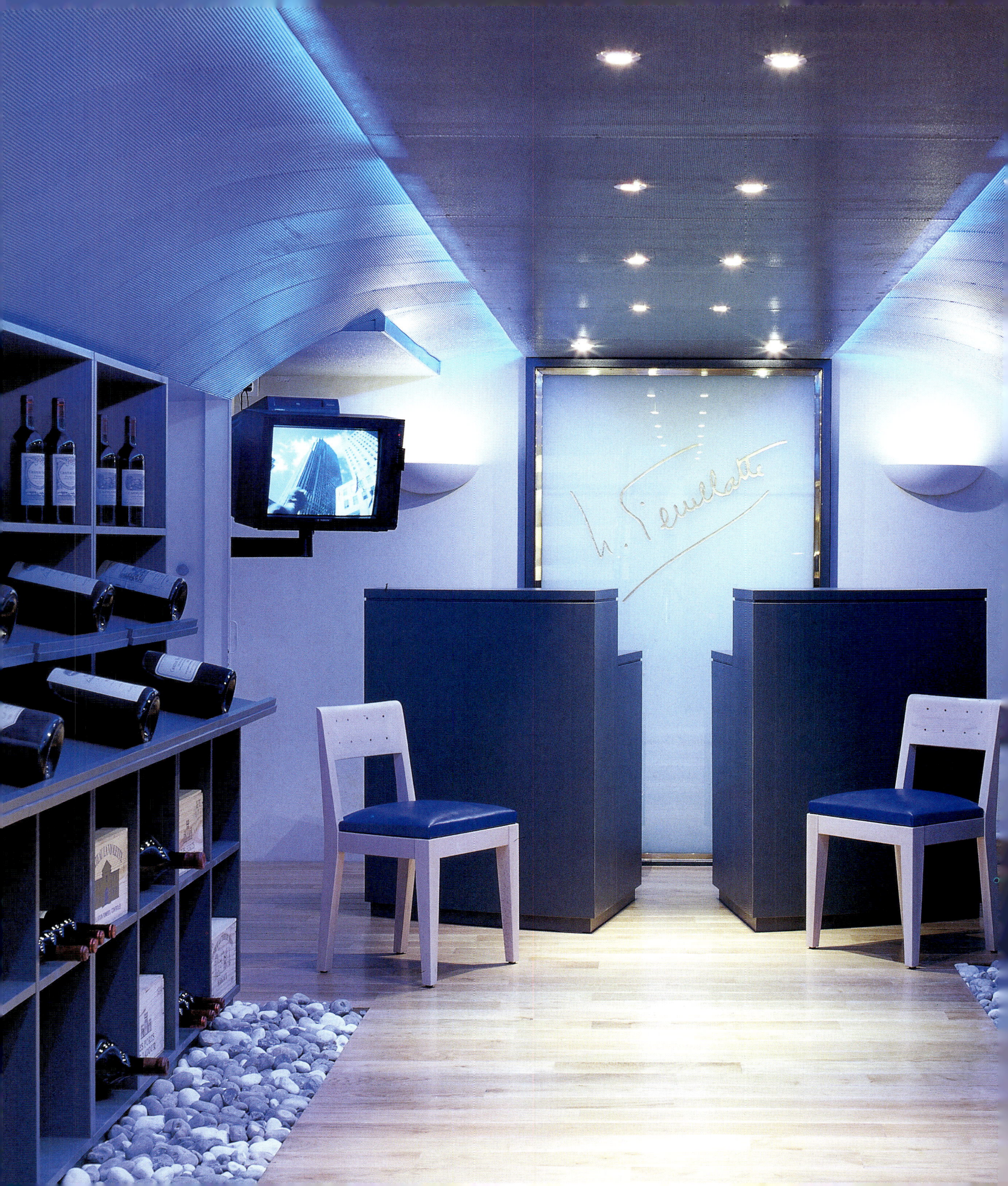

Upper: Stair detail at basement level.
Lower: Two-story column of sandblasted glass.
Opposite: Wine tasting room.

Lancel

Aix en Provence, Lille

This page: Storefront and window display.
Opposite: Limestone panels and trompe l'oeil painting in stairwell.
Overleaf: Trompe l'oeil painting and a vitrine seen from main display floor.

Lancel has manufactured exquisite leather goods since 1876, long enough for affluent customers worldwide to become devoted followers of its products. Their loyalty is well rewarded. Everything about Lancel products reveals refined design, high quality and often unique materials, and uncompromising workmanship, with each piece handcrafted in France as it has been for over 125 years. For this reason, a 1991 program to rejuvenate Lancel stores in such major markets as Paris, Lyon, Lille, Marseilles and New York included a brand identity study to ensure that the new prototype store designed by Jean-Pierre Heim (with Galal Mahmoud) would provide customers a retail experience to enhance the Lancel image. The total transformation of the Lancel store in Aix en Provence, chosen specifically for the project, began with the forms, materials and window displays on the facade, and concluded with the interior design, furnishings and display fixtures. Heim's concept called for a Minimalist space built around a major piece of trompe l'oeil art reflecting the architecture of the store. The two-story, 1,500-square-foot space in Aix en Provence was detailed as carefully as its merchandise. For example, the main stairway rising from street level to the main display floor was constructed in limestone with a crisp, geometric railing of brass and stainless steel, providing a dynamic element for a neutral backdrop of Juparana granite flooring from Brazil, limestone and plaster walls, and display cases of chestnut wood cabinetry with glass shelves and brass brackets. For color, there was furniture upholstered in yellow and red textiles and a 20-foot-high trompe l'oeil painting, executed directly on the stair wall in black ink markers and acrylic paint, depicting stairs ascending into the eternally blue Provençal sky — or wherever fine Lancel leather goods could be found.

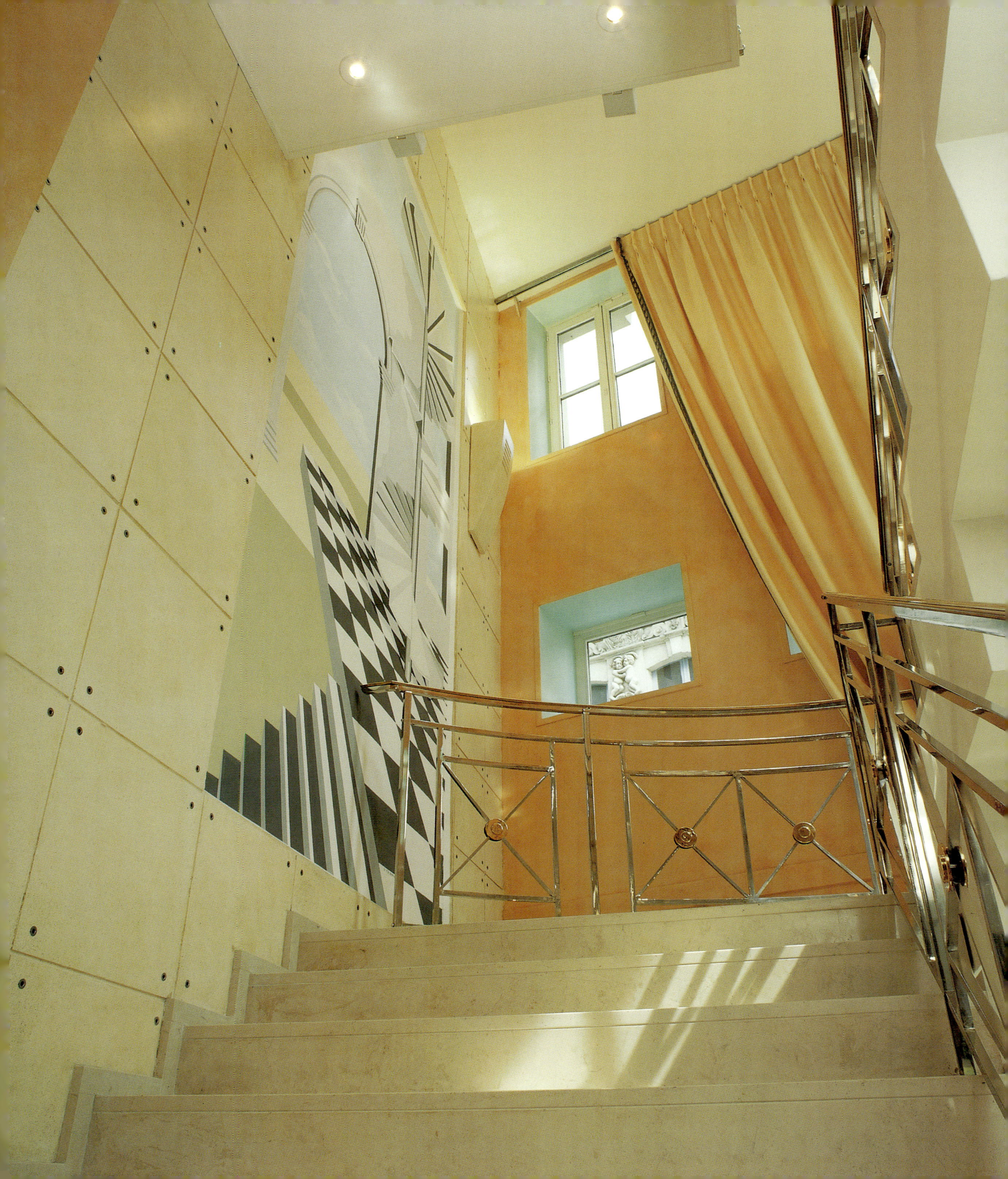

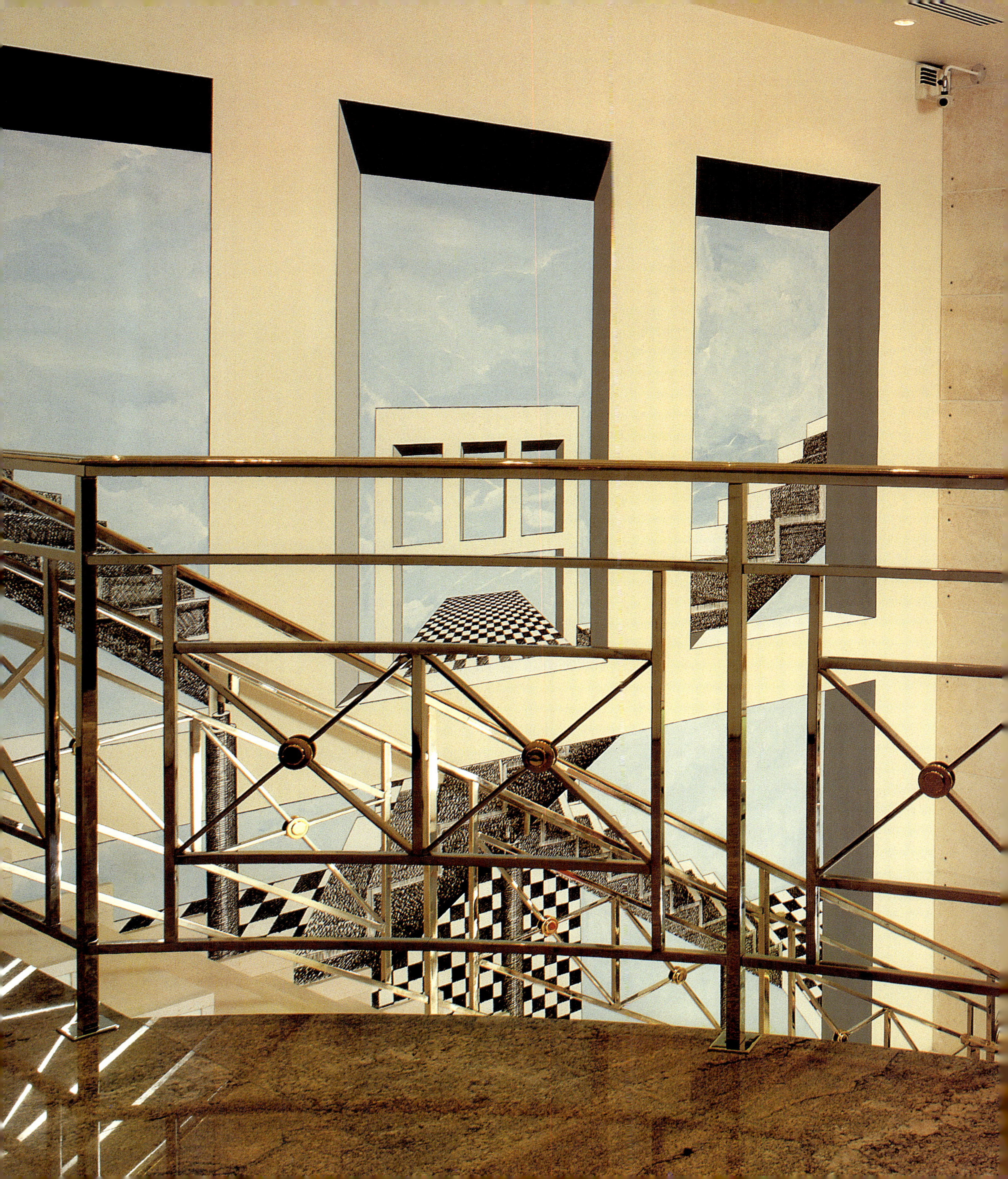

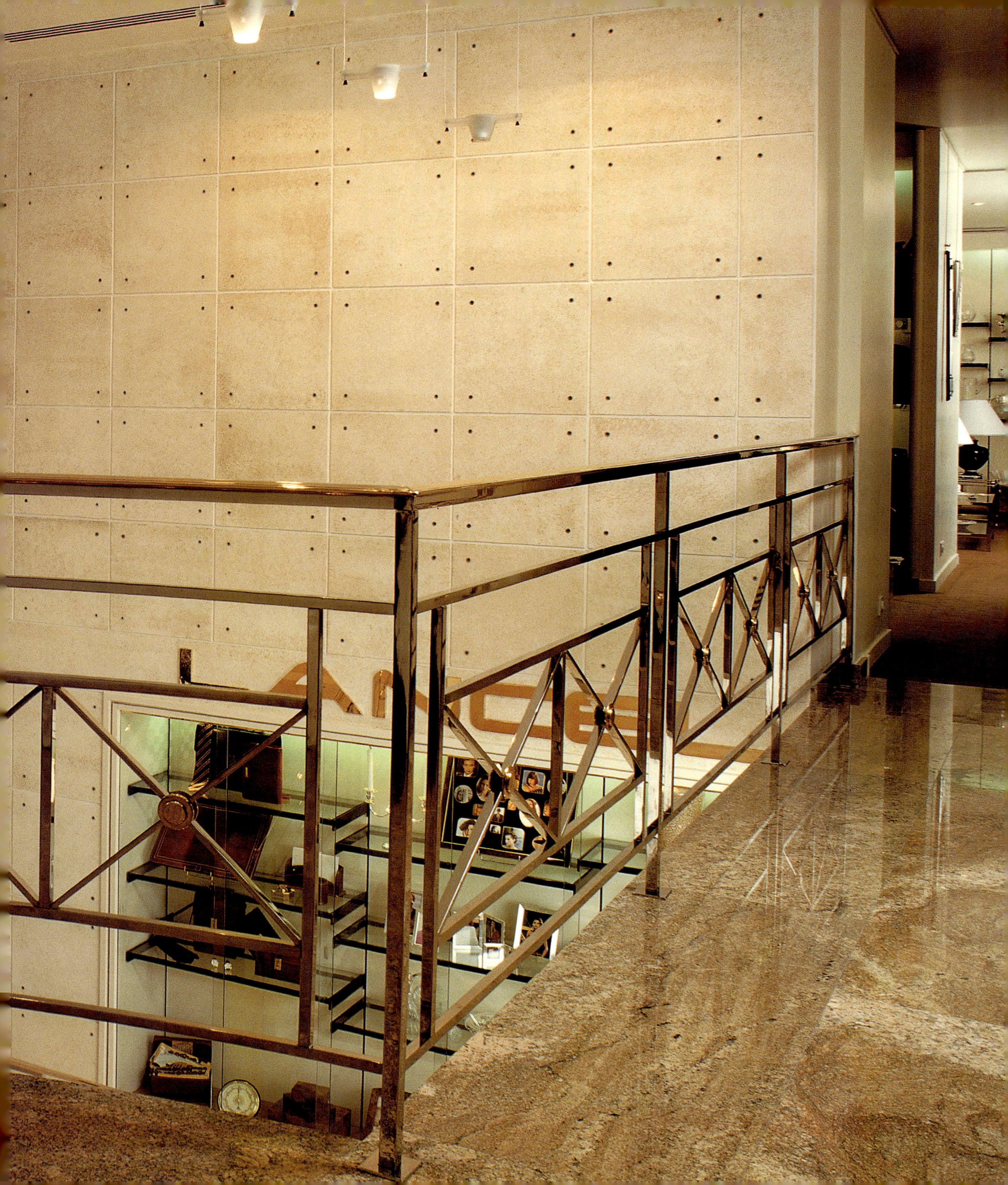

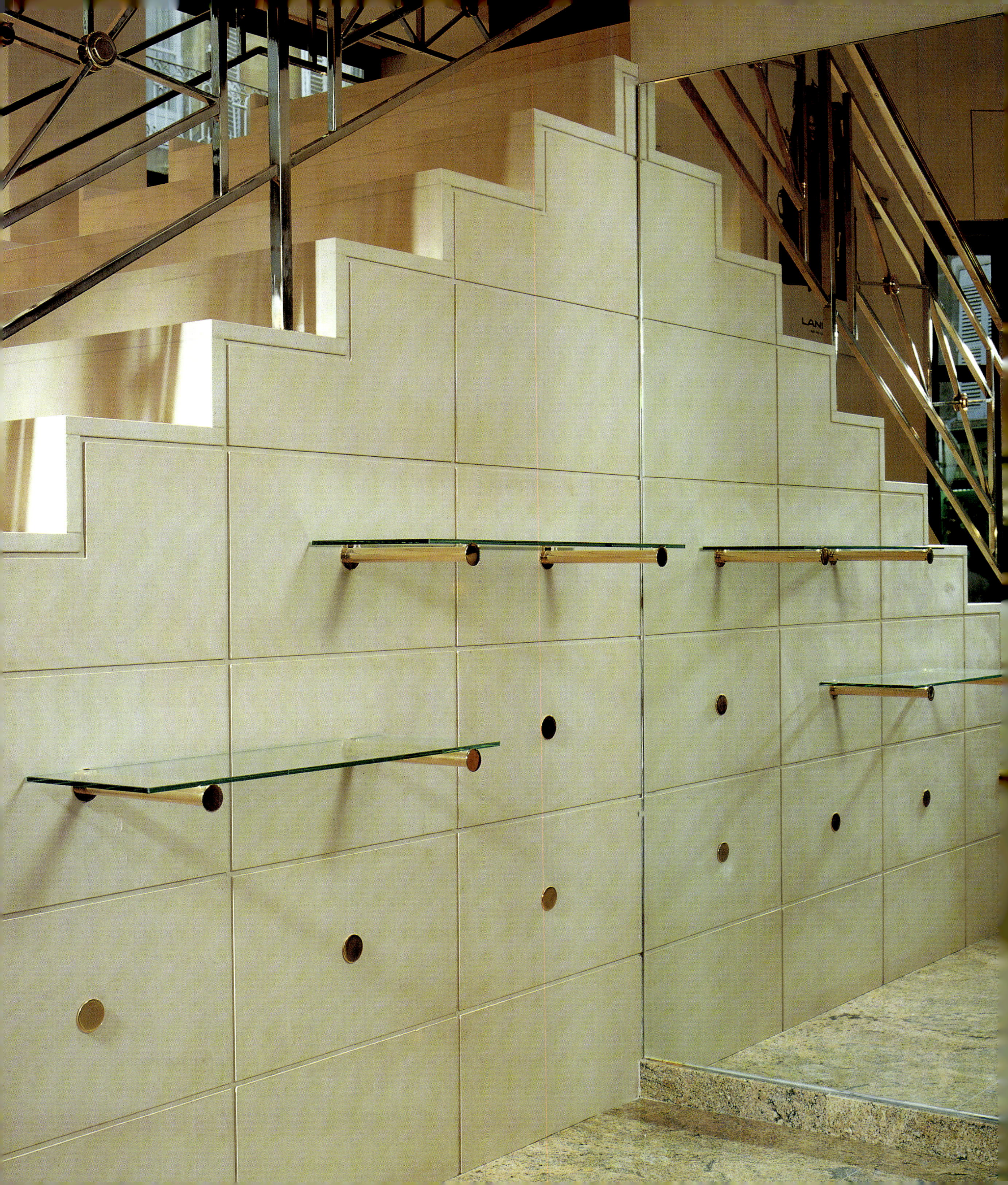

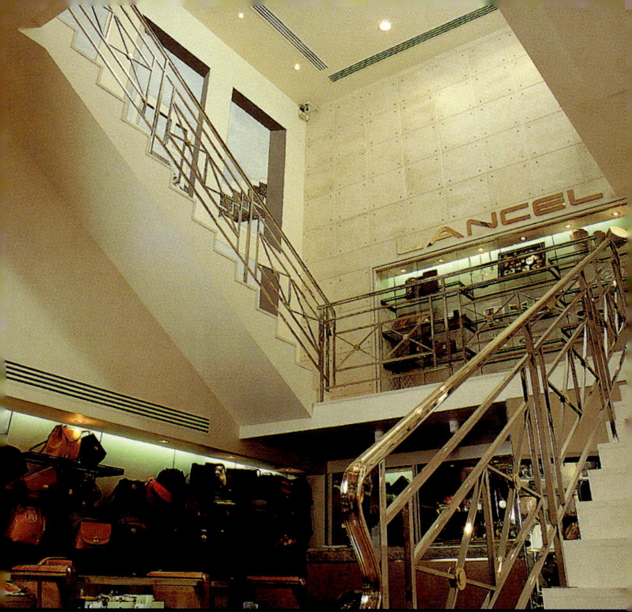
LANCEL

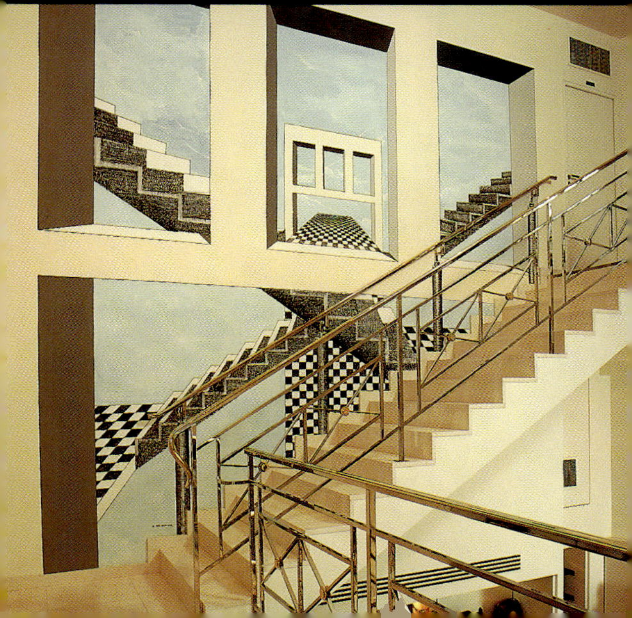

World Trade Center — Ground Zero
New York, New York USA

Who could blame New Yorkers for continuing to mourn the loss of the World Trade Center and nearly 3,000 people who perished when the twin towers fell? Nevertheless, New Yorkers, like citizens of other great cities, will renew themselves in the face of adversity. Jean-Pierre Heim's 2002 proposal for the site of the World Trade Center salutes the complex spirit of this international city with a project that simultaneously recalls the tragedy of September 11 and anticipates a better future for all. In his scheme, a 60-story, multi-functional building will occupy the site, combining a memorial to September 11 with offices, a hotel, housing, retail shops and restaurants. The structure will stand on four 50-story towers that rise from the corners of a vast square to connect at the 51st story in a 10-story superstructure that is pierced by an oculus and landscaped with a quiet, rooftop garden. The cornice-like superstructure will mirror the square below and provide an opening to convey the blue light rising from ground zero to the sky that will serve as a memorial. Others features include easy subway access, a garden labyrinth for quiet contemplation, a second garden with a memorial beside the blue light, outlines of Towers One and Two on the plaza, and red, white and blue fiber optics emanating from the building's corners. In the spirit of New York, Jean-Pierre Heim's proposal will be a living memorial.

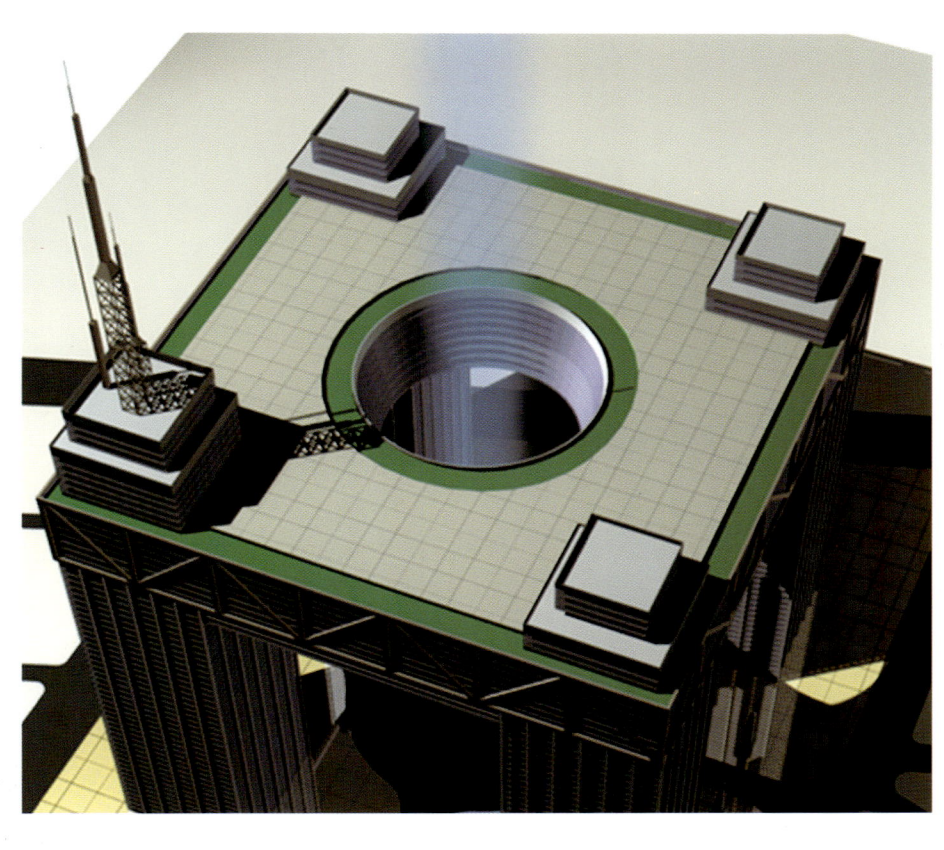

Upper: The rooftop plan, showing the oculus and blue light.
Opposite: A view of the four towers joined at the 51st story.
Overleaf: The proposal seen against the lower Manhattan skyline.

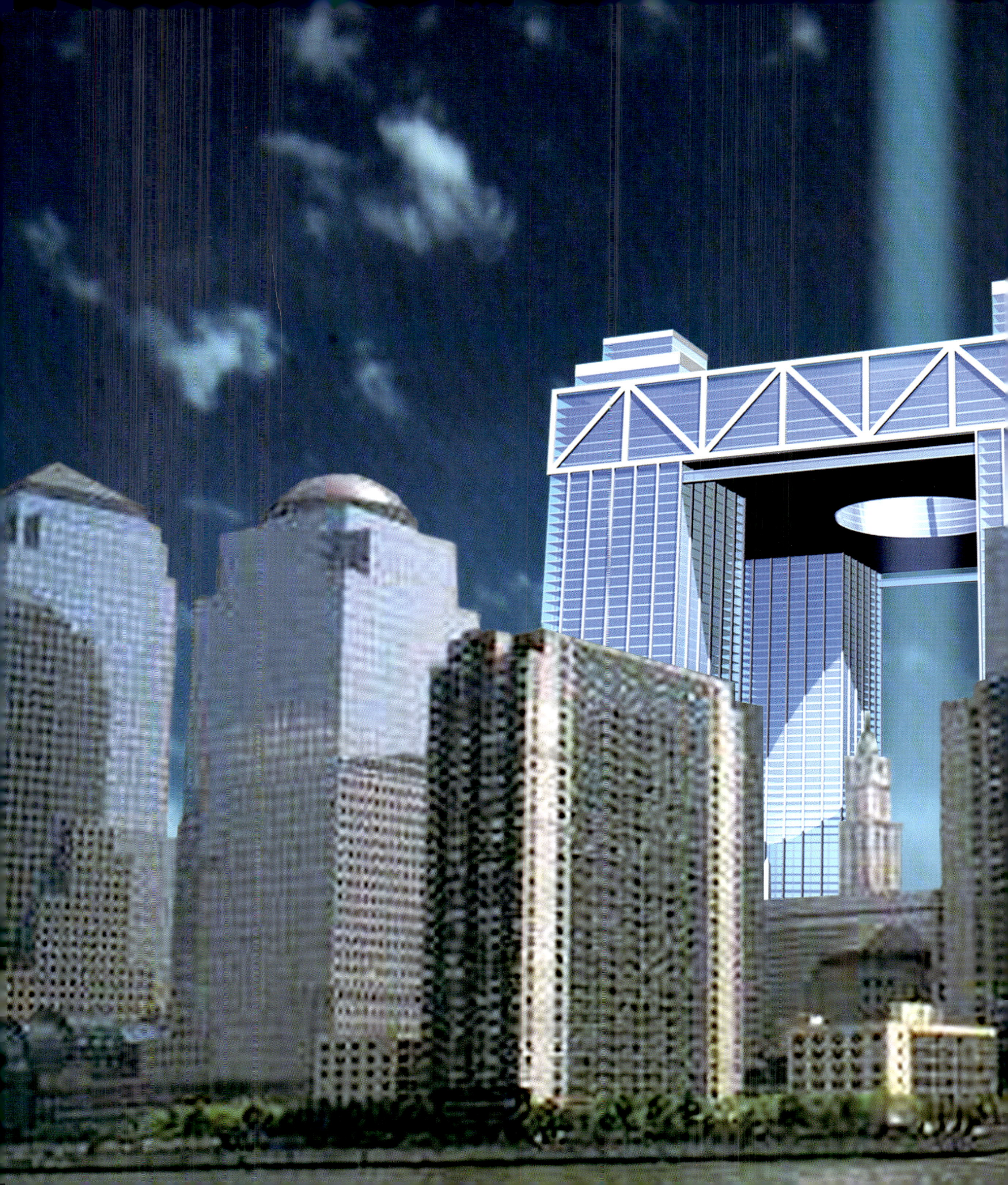

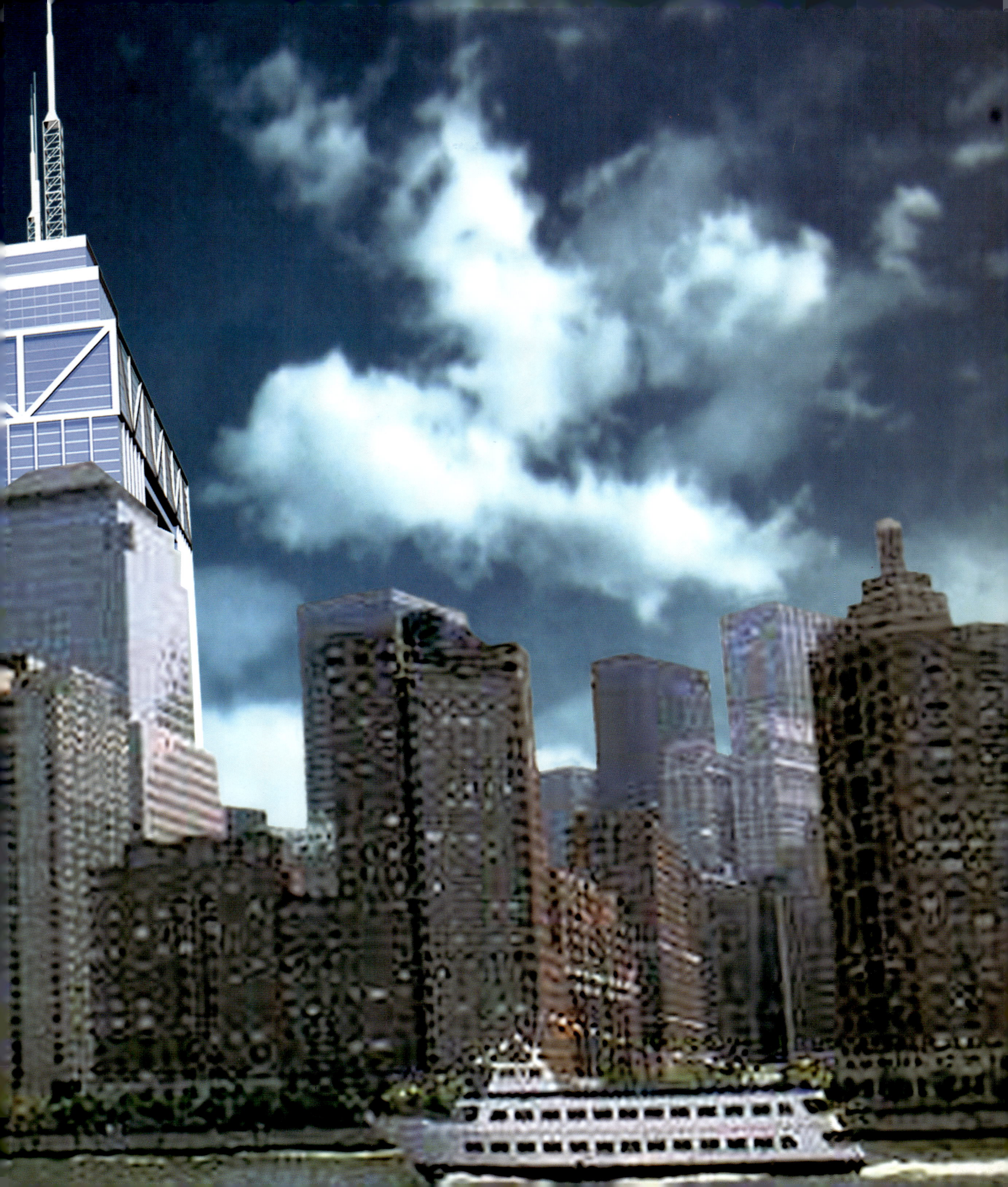

Assomption Church

Paris, France

Ask a Parisian to cite the City of Light's great churches, and he or she will readily name Nôtre Dame, Sacré-Coeur and Sainte-Chapelle. Less celebrated treasures among the city's many houses of worship seldom command this degree of attention, of course, and therein lies the tale of la Chapelle de l'Assomption. Consecrated in the 16th Arrondissement by the Archbishop of Paris in 1890, the handsome, Romanesque Revival church observed its centennial with no attempt to reverse its deterioration. Fortunately, when conditions forced the church and its affiliated school to act in 1999, Jean-Pierre Heim agreed to participate in a pro-bono assignment to rescue the 1,000-square foot edifice. Detailed studies conducted by Heim with the aid of Sister Thérèse Agnès and the church's nuns identified what had to be done, and he enlisted a crew of gifted artisans to refurbish the sanctuary. Six months later, the congregation and diocese expressed their gratitude to Heim and his colleagues for renewing their spirit and the precious building that shelters them.

This page: The galleries and clerestories in the narthex.
Opposite: A view of the nave and chancel.

ADDVCENTVR
REGN ANG
LES: A L'AMOUR QUE VOUS AUREZ LES UNS POUR LES AUTRES

Il leur répondit : « Prenez-moi, jetez-moi

r the chancel.
t wide cross, newly
s the focus of the altar.

A CECI TOUS VOUS RECONNAÎTRONT POUR MES DISCIPLES: A L'AMOUR QUE VOUS AUREZ LES UNS POUR LES AUTRES

**Paris City Hall
XVIII Arrondissement**
Paris, France

By the time engineer Gustave Eiffel built Paris City Hall in the 18th Arrondissement in 1890, he had completed what would become the city's best known monument, the tower bearing his name. Ironically, his greatest achievement was not unanimously admired by the artists and writers of the time. Though Eiffel boasted, "France will be the only country in the world with a 300-meter flagpole," Charles Garnier, Guy de Maupassant, Leconte de Lisle, Charles Gounod and others signed a protest against the Eiffel Tower. Fortunately, Paris City Hall, another artifact of the Third Republic, aroused no such controversy, having dutifully conformed to the city's reorganization into 20 Arrondissements with broad thoroughfares by Baron Haussmann two decades earlier. Conscious of City Hall's landmark status, Jean-Pierre Heim recently undertook a three-phased renovation, encompassing the facade and lobby, the main administrative chamber, and the second floor administrative offices, to simultaneously preserve Eiffel's industrial look and modernize the facilities. Key elements of the project, which divided the interior into public zones and administrative zones, included a huge skylight installed as part of a new atrium that features a mezzanine and long pedestrian bridge spanning the public area to connect numerous offices, new counters for administrative reception and other public functions, and the updating of individual rooms using modern building systems and new finishes, furniture and lighting. As a commemorative gesture, Heim also created a 25-foot-high trompe l'oeil painting beneath the new skylight. If the renovation includes a visible symbol of the pride that the people of Paris and all of France feel about the City of Light, it can be found in the main administrative chamber, where Heim has introduced the colors of Paris and France to highlight the architecture, resulting in a new name for the space, namely the Flag Room. Thanks to this timely refurbishment, the futuristic vision of Gustave Eiffel will keep watch over Paris for many more years to come.

121

French Trade Office

New York, New York USA

How should French commerce represent itself in New York, America's business center? For Jean-Pierre Heim, creating the French Trade Office for the French Embassy with architect Tyrone Roper meant developing a functional space with a strong image. (It is now regarded as a model for French Trade Offices in other cities around the world.) Thus, the visitor arriving on the 38th floor of the Trade Office's building instantly sees a back-lighted image of the U.S. and French flags in the main entry hall. The sense of a street-level office is introduced at the same time through a system of circulation spaces that are treated as "streets and avenues," starting with the carpet and ceramic tile bordering the main entry hall. From there, France, described by walls, colonnades and trompe l'oeil paintings, seems just a few symbollic steps away.

This page: The U.S. and French flags in the main entry hall.
Opposite: Circulation treated as "streets and avenues."

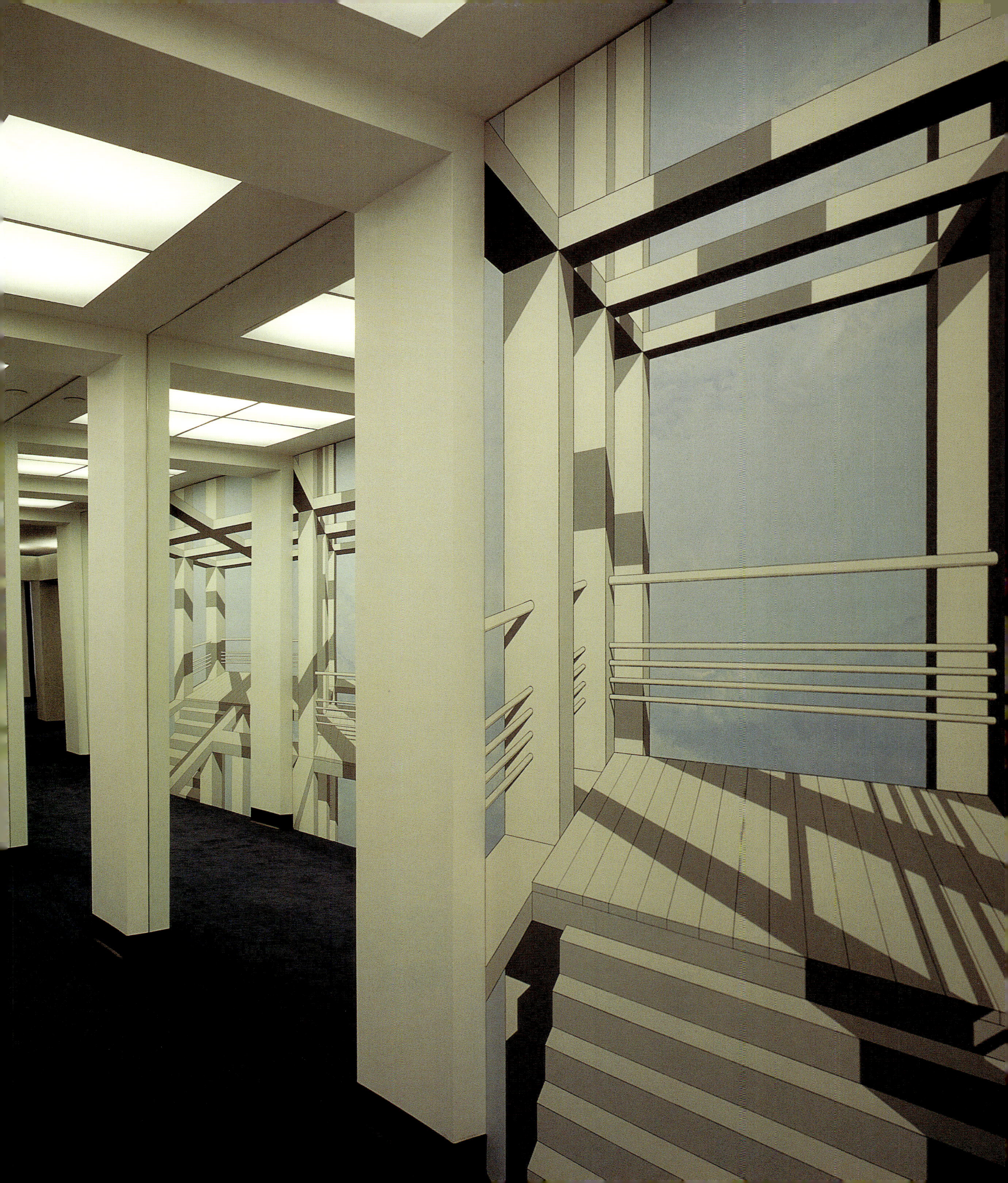

Die Leiter

Frankfurt, Germany

Visitors to Frankfurt, the powerful financial center of Germany, are pleasantly surprised to discover Frankfurters like to have fun. Excursions through the pubs, bars and restaurants of Sachsenhausen, the shops on the Goethestrasse and Fressgass, and the cultural institutions on "Museum Mile" along the Main River certainly make a convincing case. One of the informal restaurants that locals favor is Die Leiter — "leiter" means "ladder" in German — designed by Jean-Pierre Heim in 1982 and still thriving on the edge of an elegant shopping district. Having designed Frankfurt's popular Bistro 77 in 1979, Heim was pleased when its owner, Chester Sauri, gave him carte blanche to create a second bistroconcept soon thereafter.

Heim named the new restaurant "Die Leiter," which means ladder in German, in a playful allusion to the nearby opera house known as Die Alte Oper, and used a ladder as one of the performing arts motifs in its decor. Guests can spot the ladder in neon signage, as a trompe l'oeil painting and as a logo in the menu, along with such theatrical props as stage lights mounted on the ceiling, projectors that display city scenes on the walls, outsized replicas of film strips on which the daily menu is written, fake Ionic columns of paper mache, and veneers of brick and marble peeling off the bar. Like the scenery, the clientele changes with the time of day, elegant and snobbish 0yielding to witty and casual and so on, like Frankfurters on stage.

This page: Bar with brick and marble veneer.
Opposite: Study sketch for the dining room entrance.

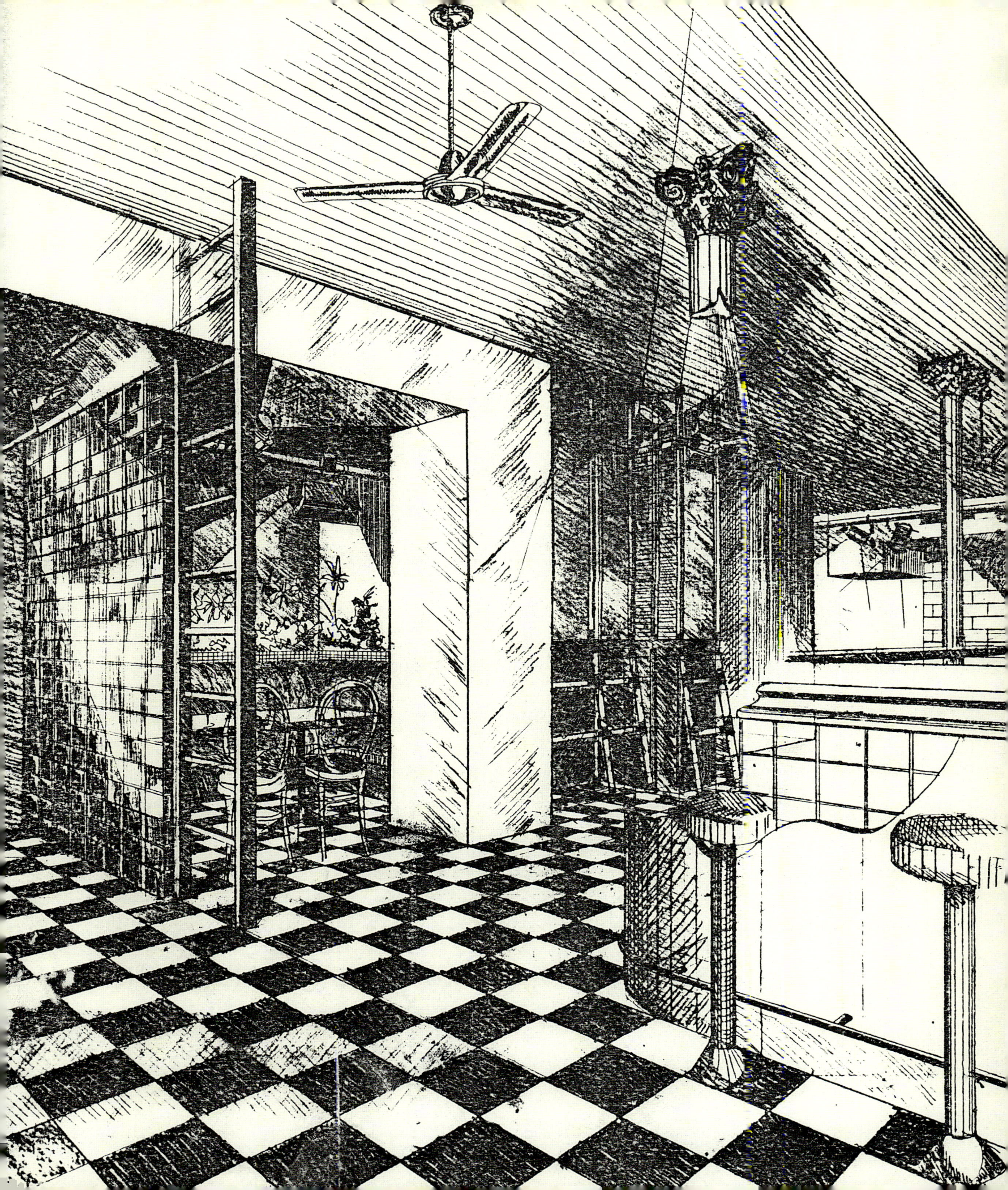

Citaix

Lyon/Nangis, France

The French know Citaix. In fact, they can expect to see one or more units of Citaix's 500-plus fleet of silver tankers flashing the company logo on the roads of France at any given moment. It's no coincidence that Citaix is one of France's major petroleum conveyors. For this reason, Jean-Pierre Heim has adopted the vehicles' high-tech look in designing the company's new headquarters near Lyon in suburban Chasse sur Rhone, and its regional office near Paris in suburban Nangis, which has counterparts in the metropolitan regions of Marseilles and Lyon. Each building's concrete structure is sheathed in a smooth skin of galvanized aluminum that deliberately contrasts with a base of rough concrete. The Minimalist approach to the

Upper: Main entrance to the headquarters.
Lower: A view of the principal facade.
Opposite: The skylight over the Chasse sur Rhone office.

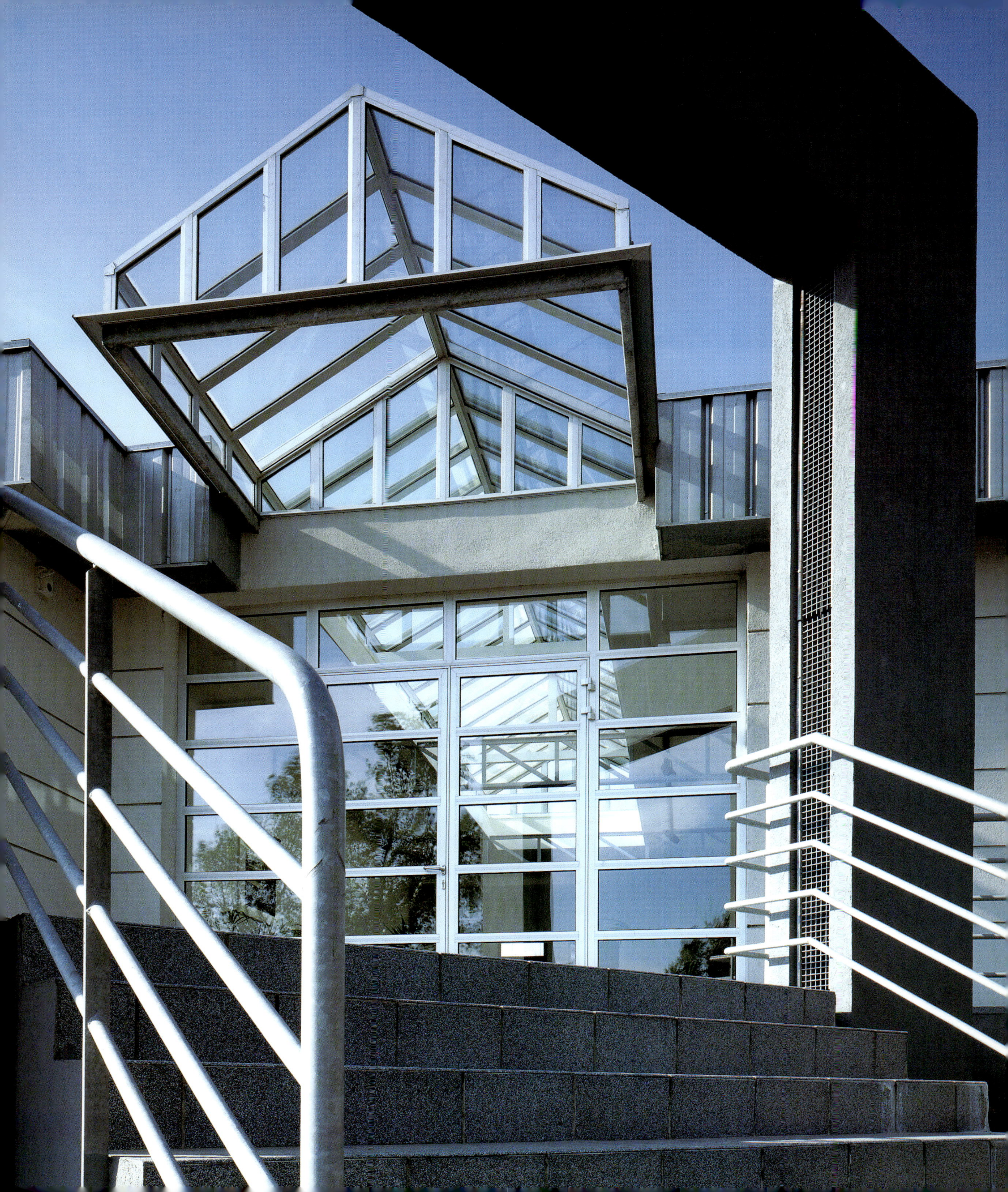

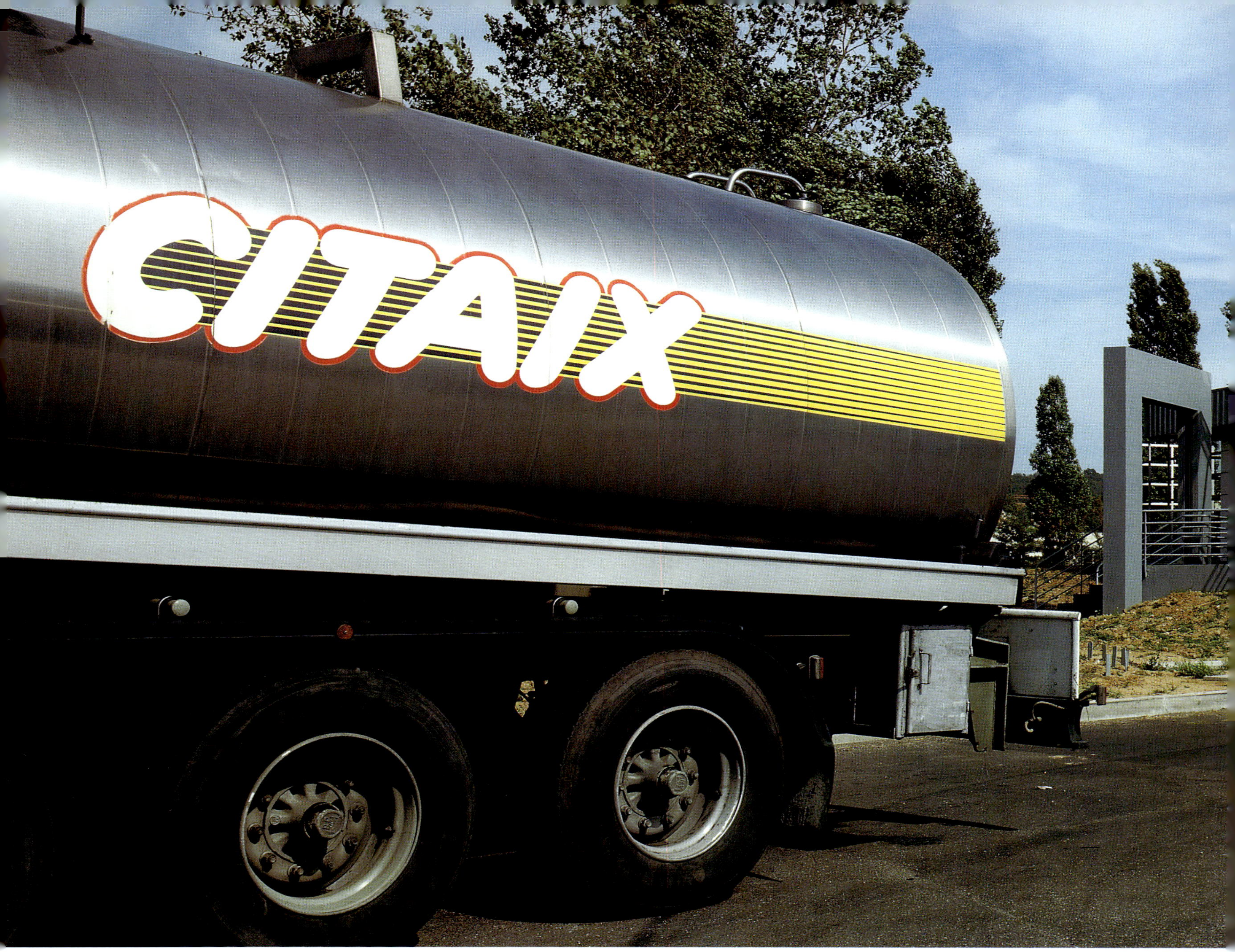
CITAIX

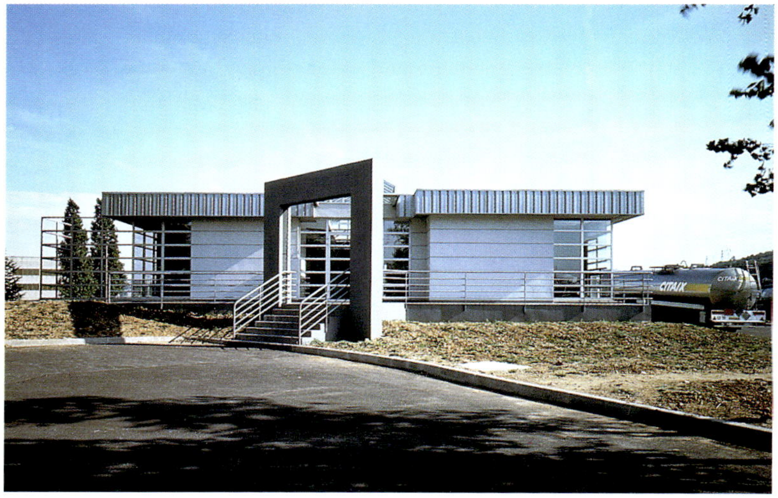
CITAIX

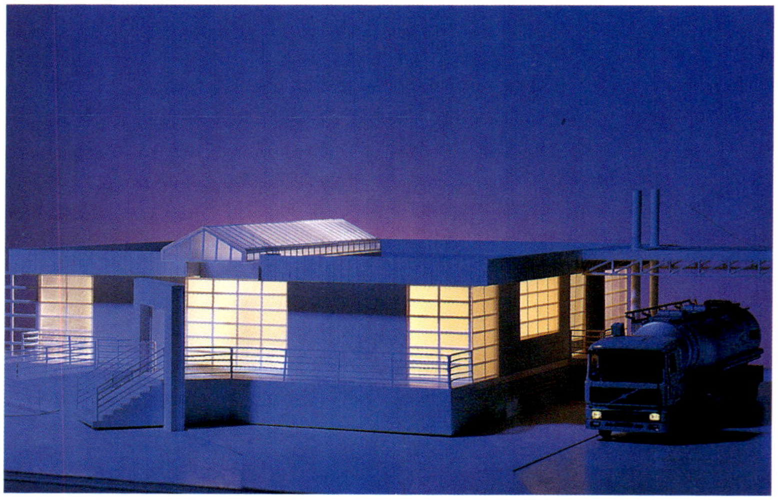

long, low buildings, which are attended by large, on-site parking lots and service aprons, gives Citaix a modern, practical and hard-working public image that suits its dynamic strategy of rapid growth and complements the two suburban locations. Past the facades, however, are two highly supportive work environments that are flooded with light from skylights over the central atriums and large windows that let workers monitor the trucks outside. The buildings even resemble the truck fleet in another, less obvious way — both are designed to expand easily to meet the growing energy requirements of Citaix's customers.

Left: Main entrance to the Chasse sur Rhone office.
Right: Model showing Chasse sur Rhone office at night.
Above: A Citaix tanker parked beside the Chasse sur Rhone office.

Trompe L'Oeil

Above: A real fireplace plays a key role in a trompe l'oeil composition in a private residence in Quoque, New York.

Have you noticed the expressions of wonder and delight on the faces of people exploring the imaginary space of virtual reality created by computers, video games and movies? Portraying three-dimensional depth in two-dimensional and three-dimensional forms may be a behavioral trait hard-wired in humanity since prehistoric painters created murals in the caves of Lascaux. In any event, artists and architects have used walls to this effect for centuries, depicting seemingly real objects that lie just beyond the grasp of our fingers, and distant panoramas that appear to stretch as far as the horizon. In the work of Jean-Pierre Heim, architectural wall perspectives have been part of his creative vision from the start of his practice. Mixing reality and illusion, he has used architectural murals to extend existing perspective lines to convergence, introduce architectural elements that may allude to distant places and times, or develop vistas that would exist as follies in our physical world. Although Heim can refer to almost any location, history and culture

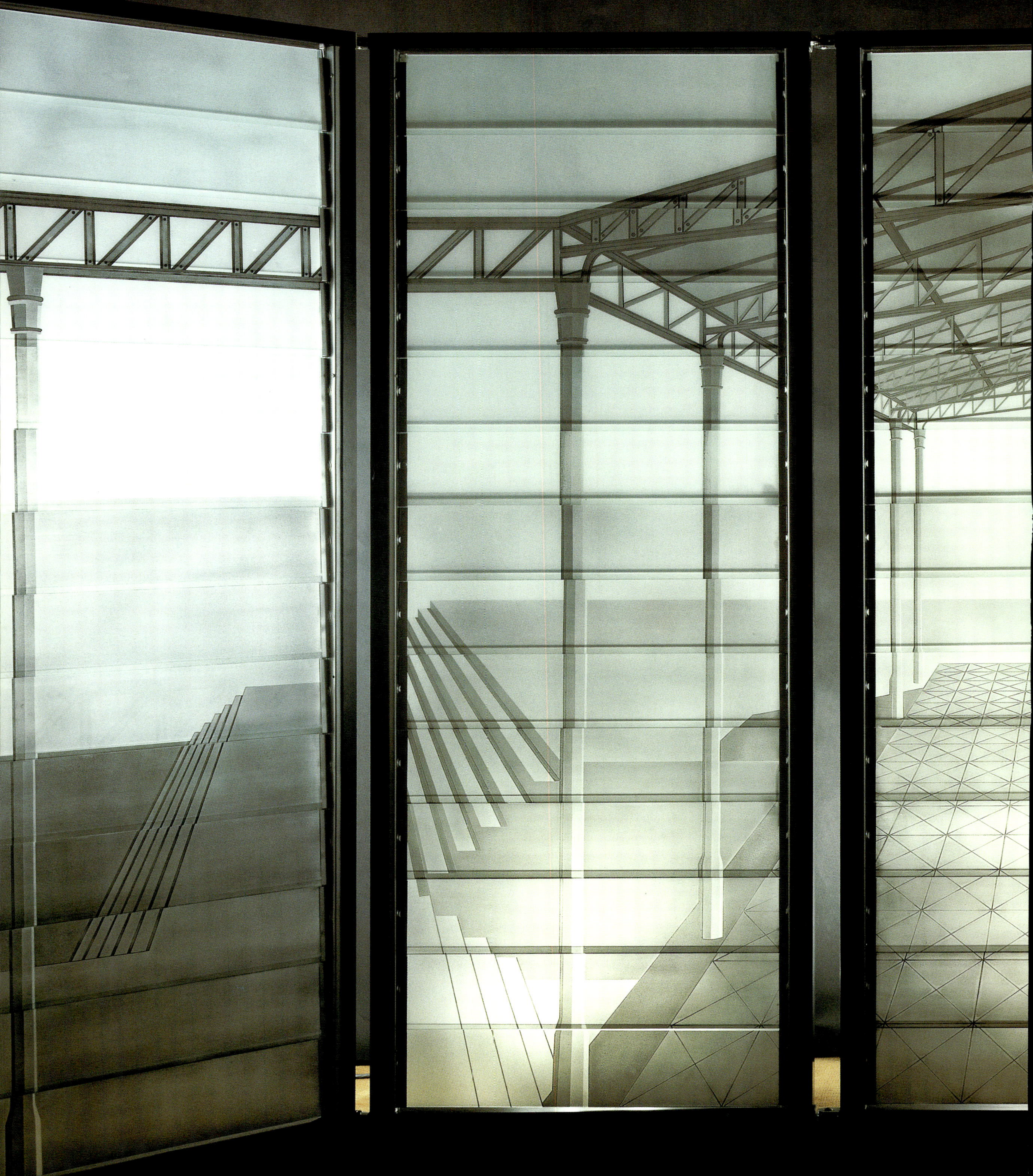

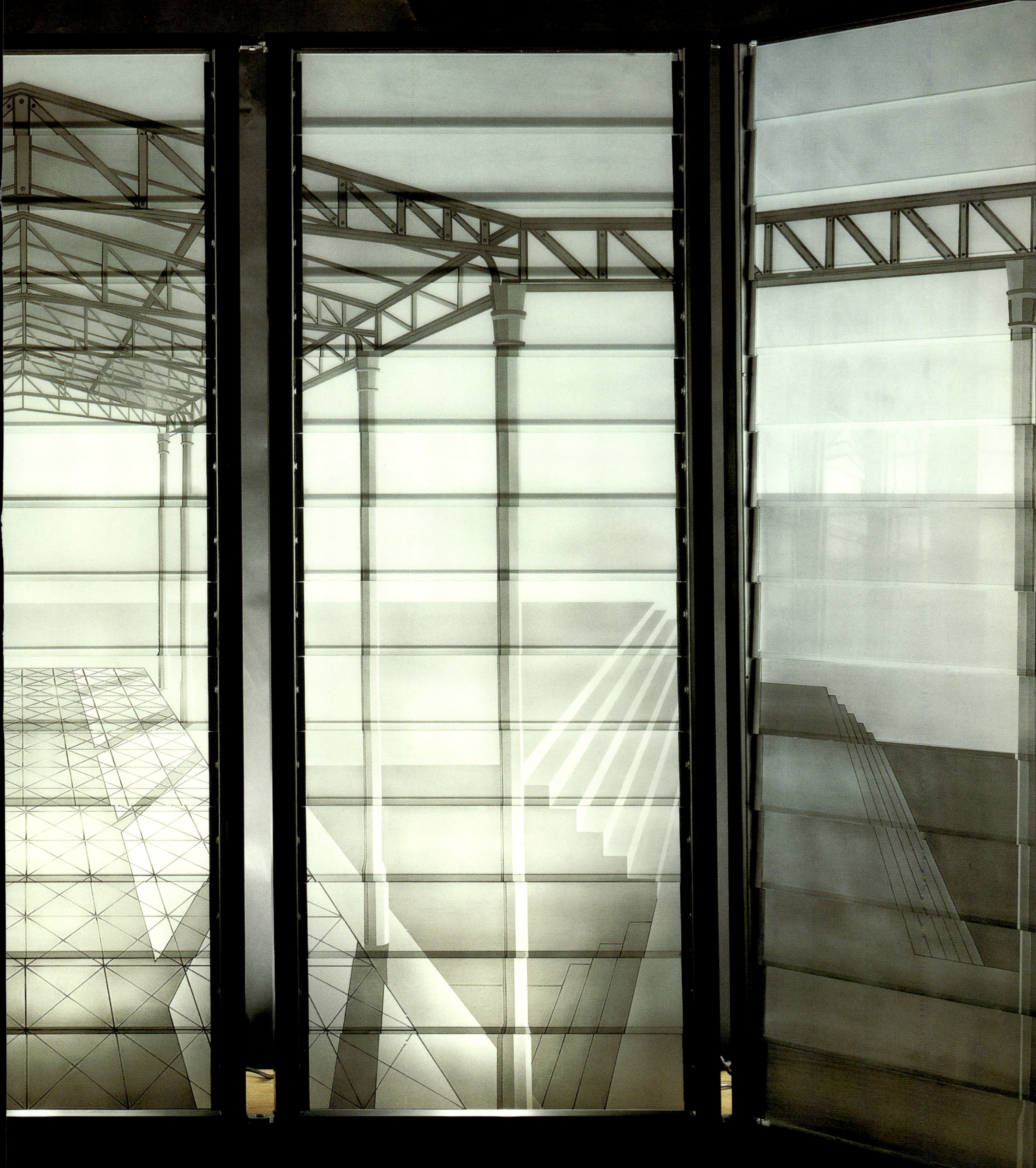

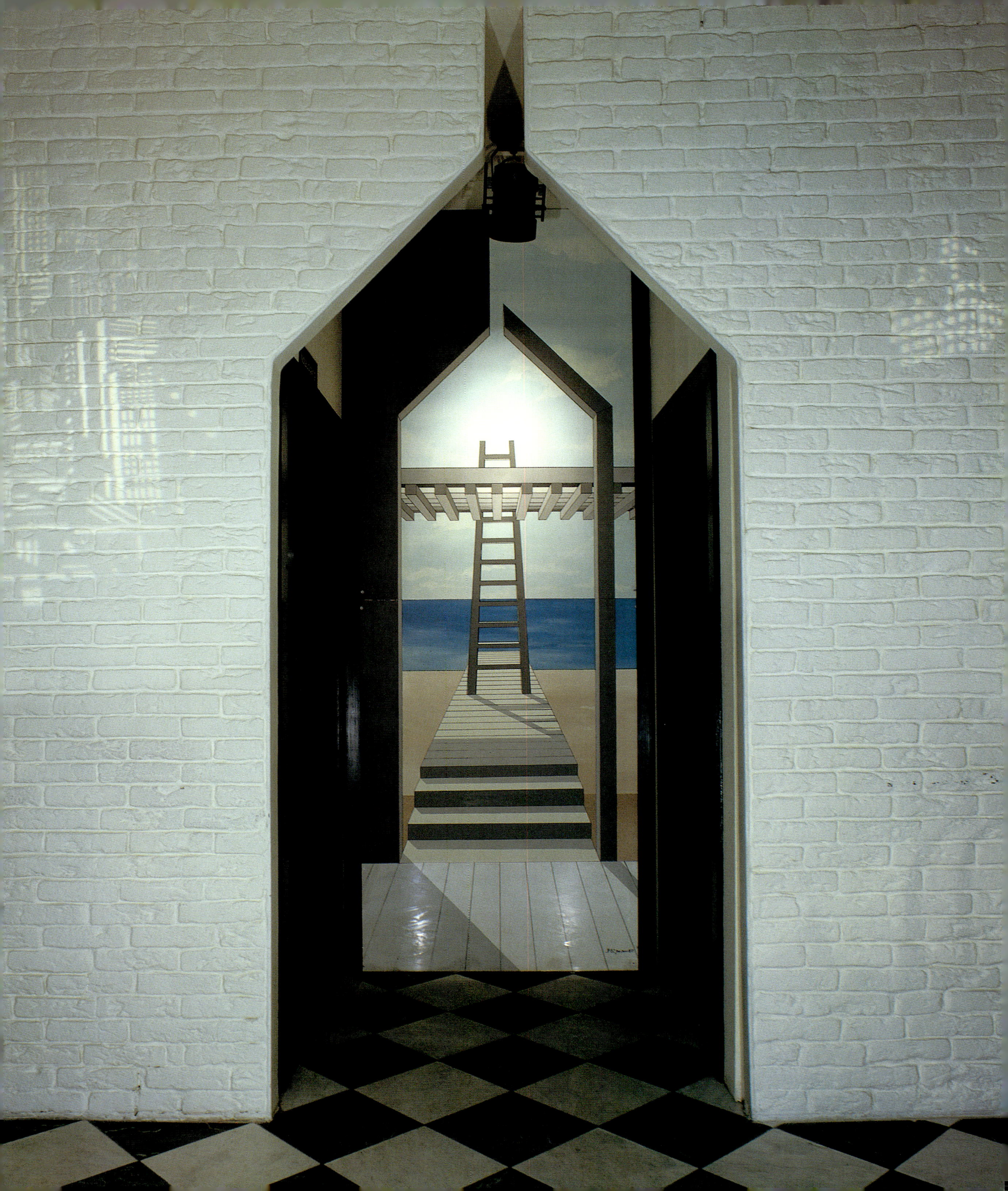

to give substance to his trompe l'oeil projects, which he develops with Christine Heim, interior designer, he is most inspired by Italian Renaissance architecture, whose fascination with trompe l'oeil and monumental forms are very sympathetic to his own interests. The ideas behind the images in his perspectives may not always be uncomplicated, yet the images themselves are mostly figurative, created with strong line drawings and simple colors so they can be appreciated by audiences at multiple levels of comprehension. Even so, Heim is not afraid to transform space with humor. In the right circumstances, a visual joke can be the best cure for a meaningless or boring wall, doorway or window view. What matters is appropriateness. Consider, for example, a contemporary glass screen designed by Jean-Pierre Heim and crafted by the workshop of Guillaume Saalburg in Paris. This very simple aluminum frame with adjustable window louvers combines technology and fantasy in a way that fascinated late 19th century architects and engineers, who created such romantic works as the Crystal Palace and the Eiffel Tower, and can still capture our attention today. Each piece of glass is individually sandblasted and colored, based on light, simple line drawings. How does the completed screen project its delicate atmosphere? That's trompe l'oeil.

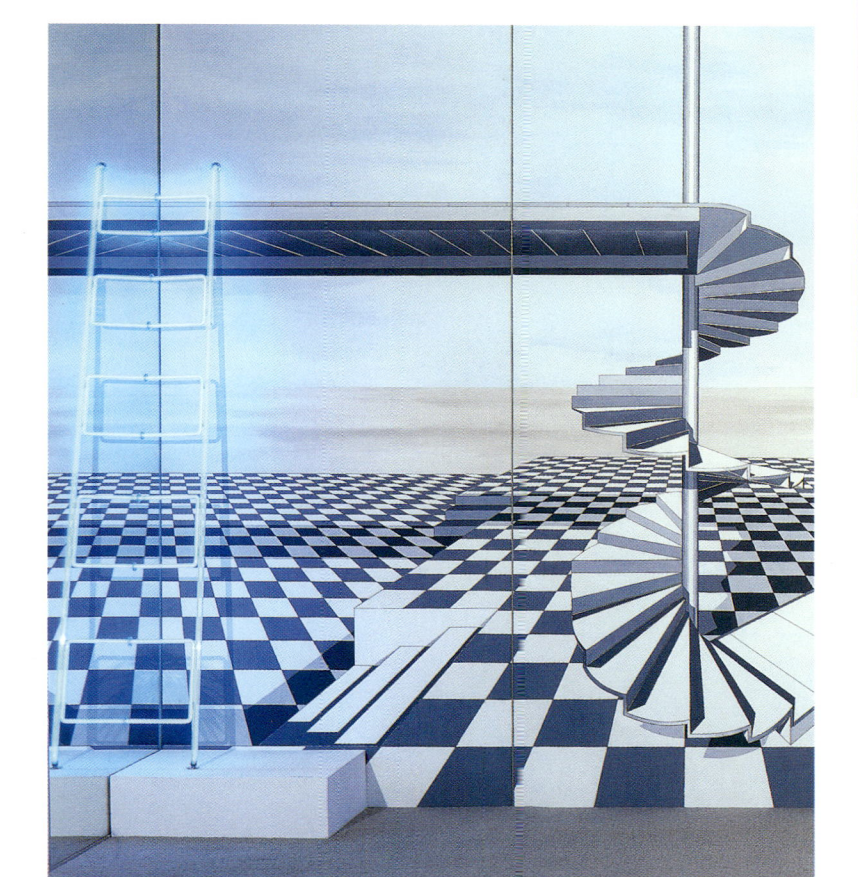

Left: Trompe l'oeil ladder in neon by Rudy Stern, manufacturer, doing business as Let There Be Neon.
Above: Three-dimensional, white-on-white sculpture entitled "la Scala Interrotta."
Top: A three-panel screen, Crystal Palace Station #2, displayed at B & B Italia's showroom exhibition in New York.
Opposite: Die Leiter, a restaurant in Frankfurt whose name means "ladder" in German, displays this trompe l'oeil ladder.

Luxor Line — Egyptian Collection

Jean-Pierre Heim's Luxor Line represents his Egyptian Collection of furniture and tableware, a tribute to Ancient Egypt that is also a reaffirmation of the French passion for Egyptian antiquities that began when Napoleon led a 35,000-man expeditionary force to Alexandria in 1798 and became enraptured with the nation. The designs by Heim for furniture, porcelain dinnerware, silverware, table linen, candles, vases and lamps balance the Ancient Egyptian devotion to graceful, minimal profiles and solid, monolithic forms with the needs of contemporary living. The products are being created with established purveyors of luxury goods such as Bernardaud, the manufacturer of Limoges, for the fine china, Odiot for the silverware, Porthault for the linen, Point a la Ligne for the candles, and Glass by Murano for the vases and lamps. They will be available to the public through gift shops and museum stores, reassuring customers that while the Little Corporal was not successful in holding onto Egypt, his grip on its decorative arts and crafts remains firm in the capable hands of his successors.

Upper: Silverware from Odiot.
Lower: An occasional table crafted in ebony.
Opposite: A pendant lighting fixture from Glass by Murano
is suspended over an occasional table of ebony.
Overleaf: A sampling of tableware from the Luxor Line.

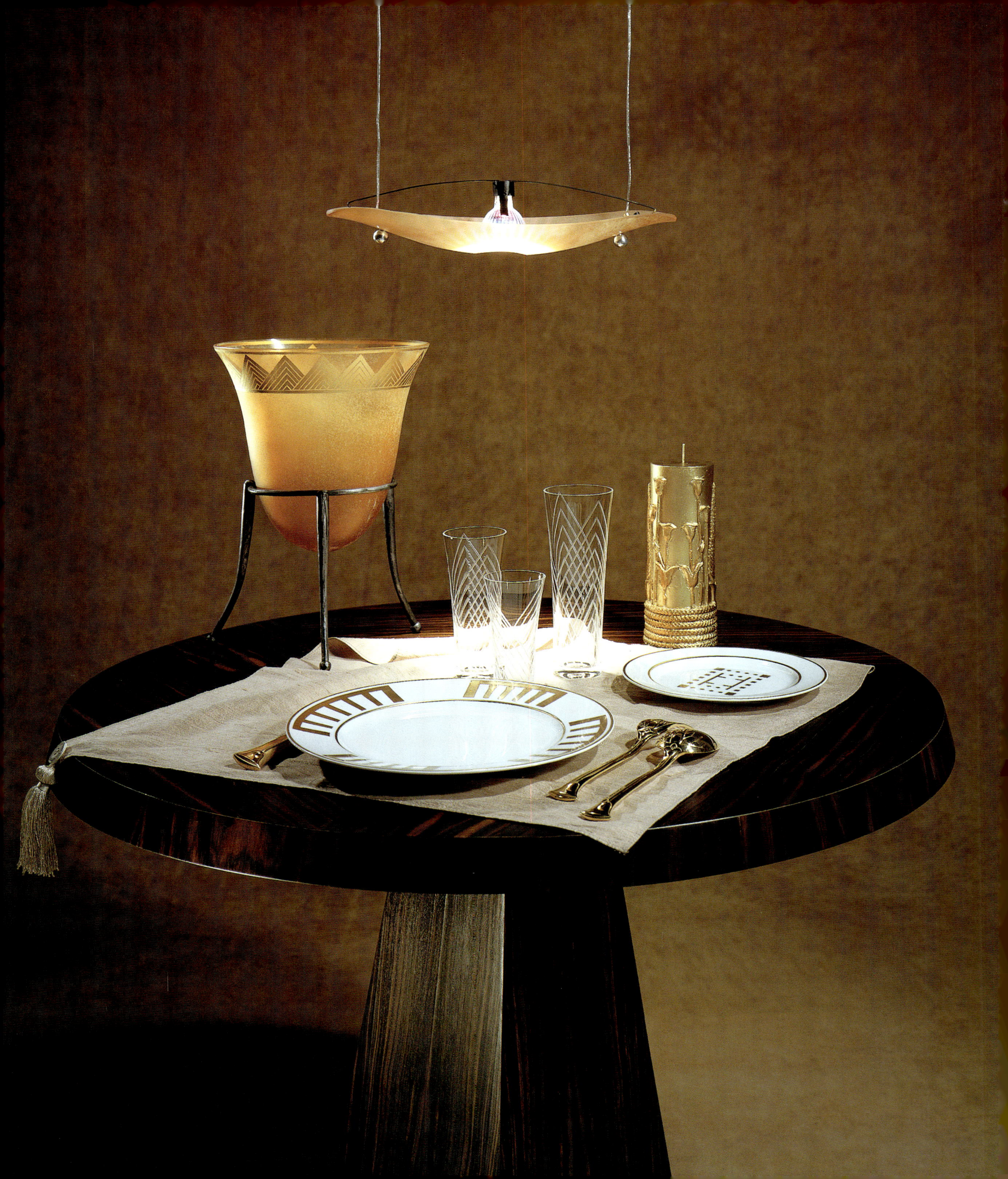

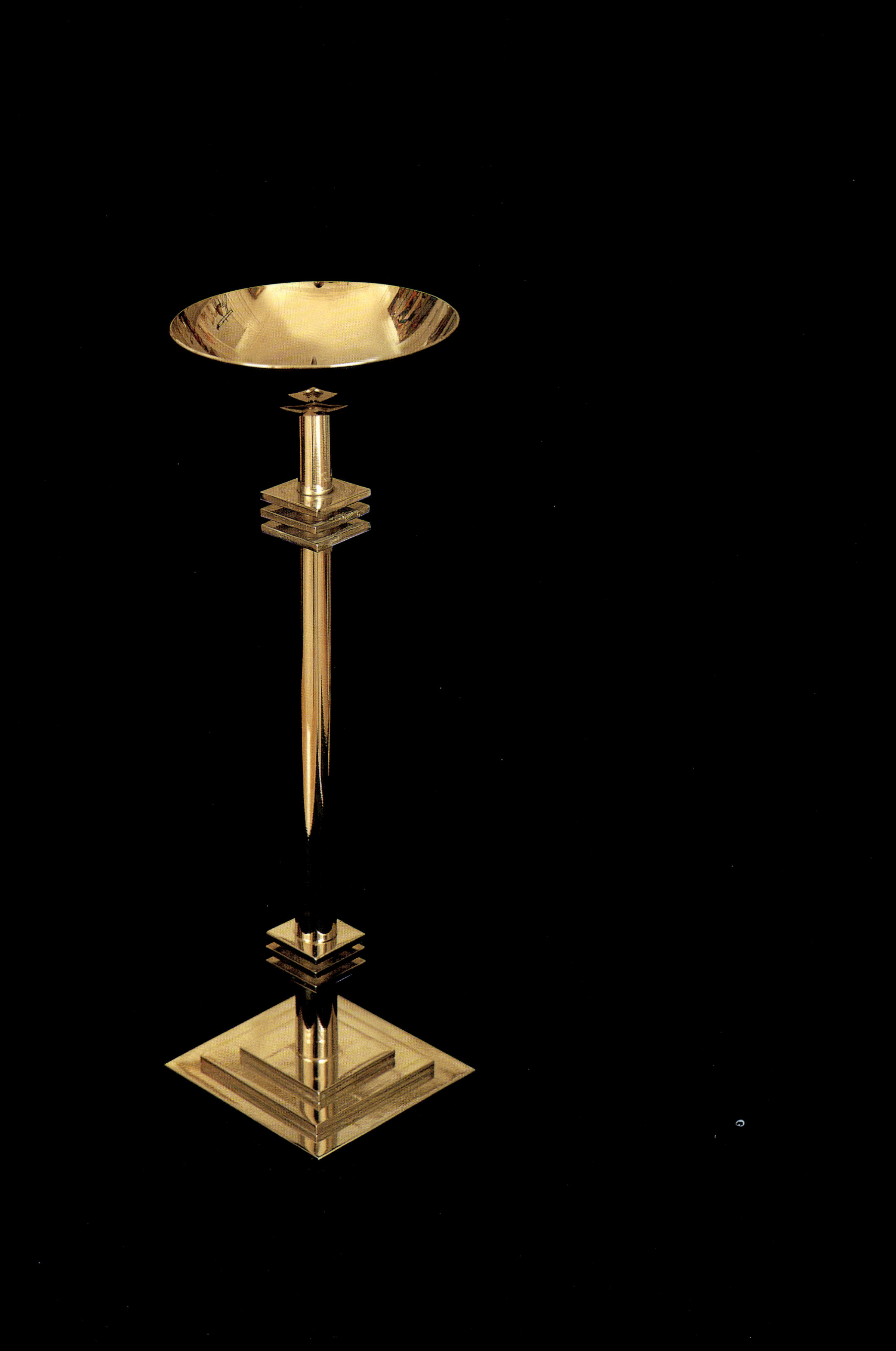

Furniture Line

One reason why architects like to design furniture, as many practitioners will happily admit, is that furniture pieces resemble miniature buildings that can be completed with less time, manpower and other resources than buildings require — especially if their appeal lies in artistry and craftsmanship rather than technology and automated production. Another justification is that custom furniture design helps to create a totally consistent and responsive environment for a client, embracing everything outside and inside a building. A third excuse, if one were needed, is the obvious aesthetic achievement that well-designed furniture can represent in terms of forms, materials and functions. Jean-Pierre Heim designs furniture to provide the best possible projects for his clientele. Using such attractive and enduring materials as bleached light oak, leather and woolen textiles, he designs chairs, benches, dressers, desks and other tables that are shaped and sized to fit the interiors they

This page: Chairs crafted in bleached oak and dyed leather.
Opposite, above: Occasional table with storage drawers.
Opposite, below: Bench with storage behind pivoting doors.

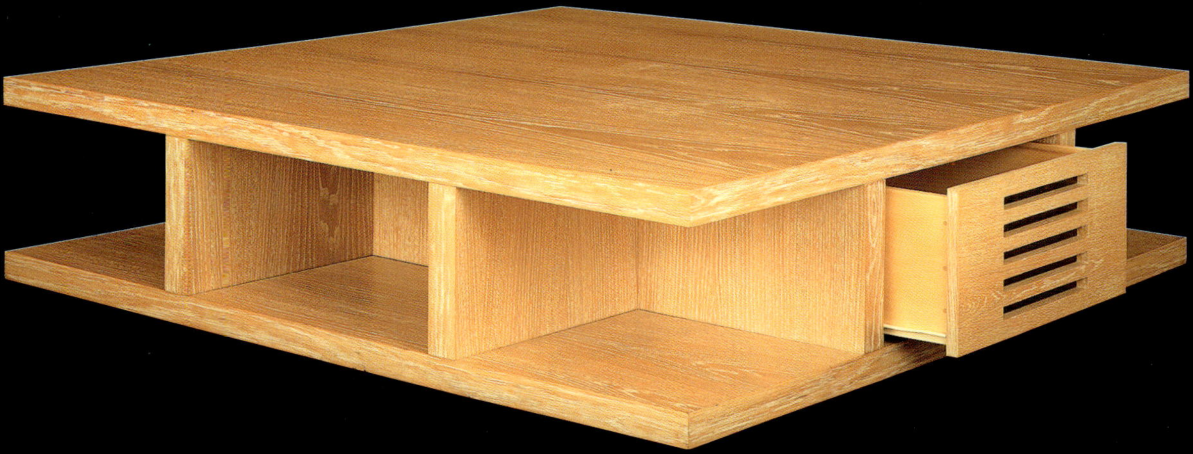

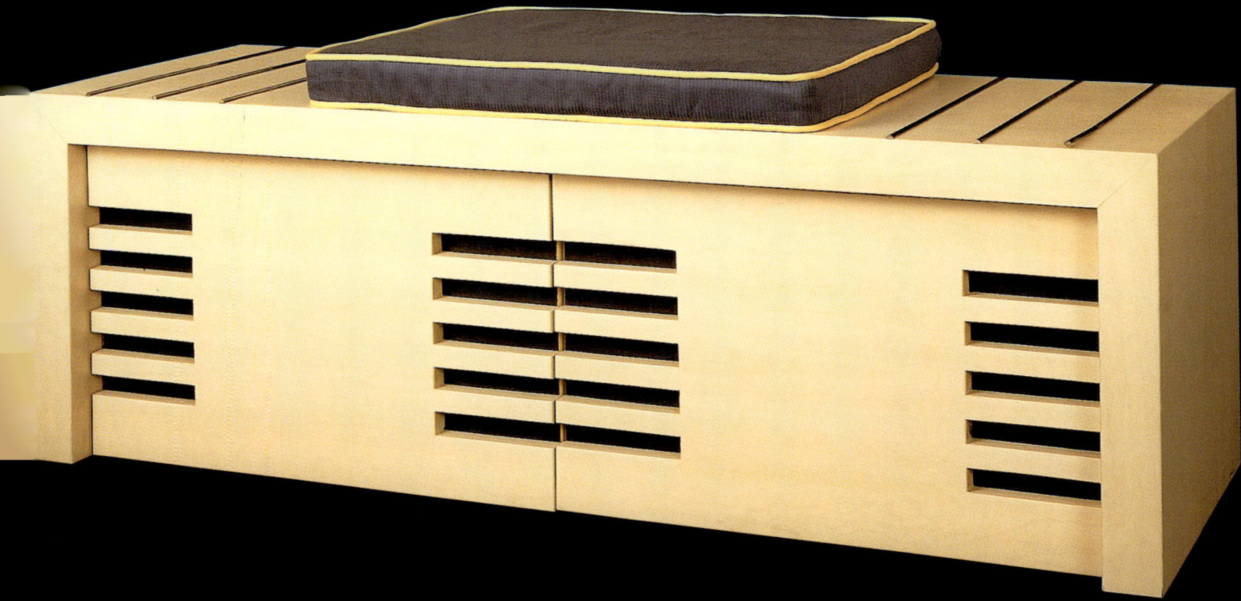

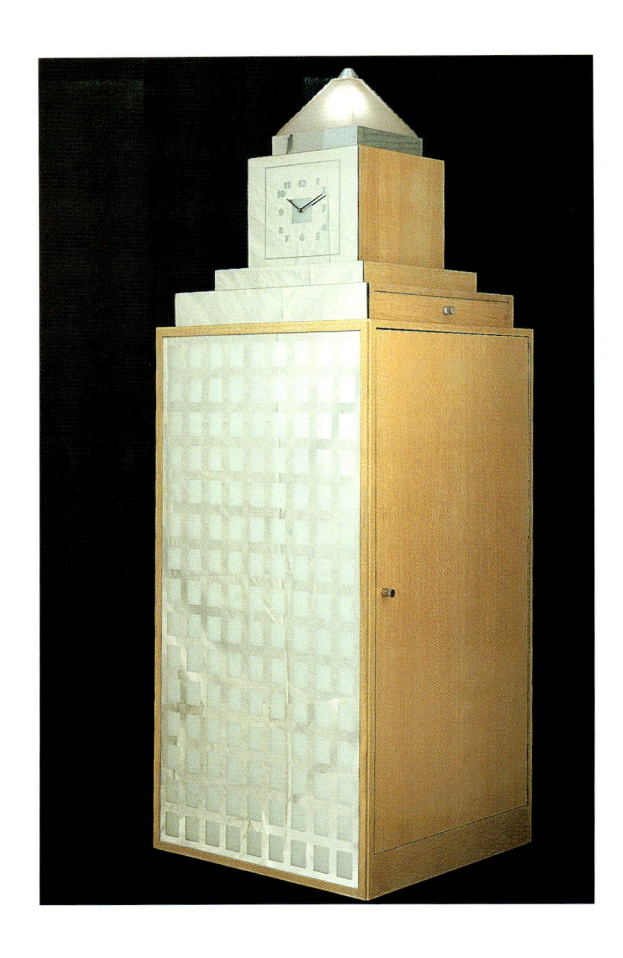

Upper: Multi-functional man's bedroom cabinet for jackets, pants, shirts, ties, shoes and belts with integrated clock radio, light fixture and mirror.
Lower: The same multi-functional man's bedroom cabinet in wood and metal, exhibiting the doors and drawers used for various wardrobe articles.

will furnish and the people they will serve. The dynamic and simple lines of his furniture leave room for special details, such as sliding extensions to raise the capacity of dining tables, low backs for seating that enhance the size of the rooms they occupy, and dresser drawers for men's shirts. Colors and finishes are also available to be used in giving a strong identity to a room or an entire facility that can reinforce a client's branding and other marketing activities. Whatever a client's requirements may involve, Jean-Pierre Heim is ready to custom ers value in ways that standard, mass-produced furniture cannot easily match.

Above and below: Studies for variations n the detailing and finish of the multi-functional man's bedroom cabinet, including elevations and sections.

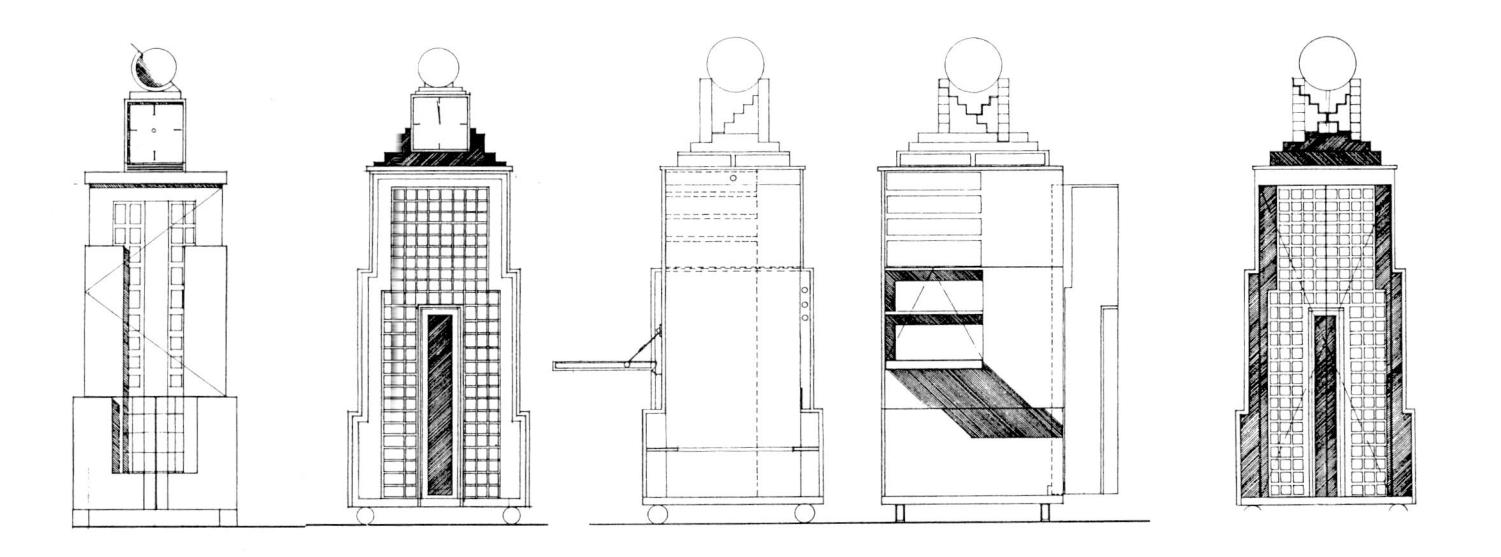

Apartment — Paris I

Paris, France

A glance through French interior decorating magazines reveals the power of tradition as one Parisian residence after another reprises the dark, heavy and historical setting celebrated in the art of Degas, Toulouse-Lautrec and Vuillard. Yet more contemporary-minded families want livelier alternatives, such as the 4,000-square-foot apartment designed by Jean-Pierre Heim in a 1930s building. Seeking a Mediterranean ambiance of simple colors and abundant light, the elements that attracted Matisse to the south of France, Heim made such critical changes to the existing apartment as reconfiguring the top floor and servants' quarters, removing walls to combine the living room, dining room and entrance hall in a continuous space separated by classical columns and contrasting floor materials, and removing the living room ceiling to double its height, display a new balcony on the upper floor and simulate a courtyard. To enhance the openness, Heim left windows uncovered, installed mirrors and modern furnishings, and painted trompe l'oeil murals depicting perspectives and the sky. The result: a contemporary home for a contemporary family.

Upper: Trompe l'oeil mural in the dining room.
Lower: A perspective from the living room.
Opposite: The entrance hall view of the living room.

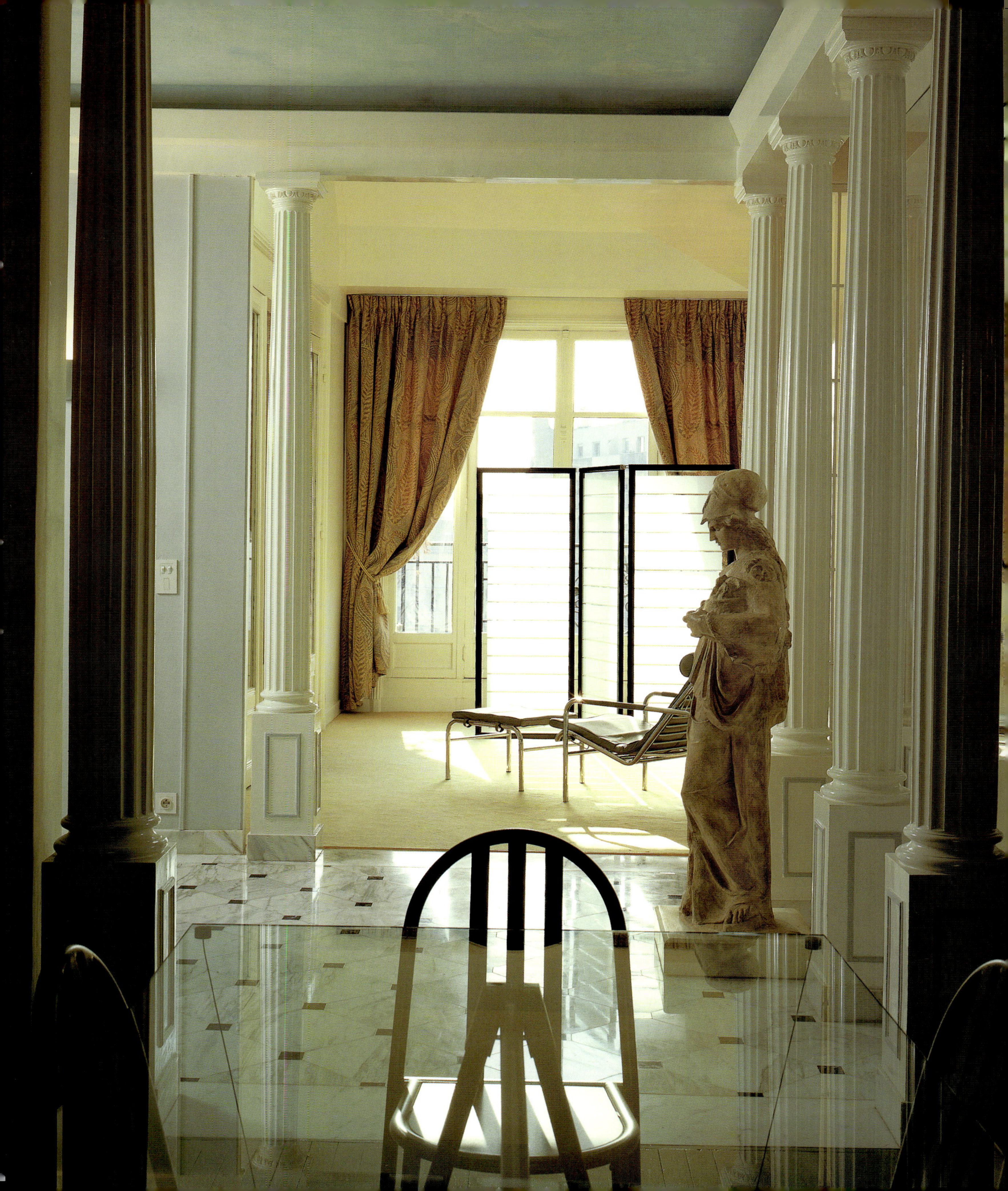

Apartment — Paris II

Paris, France

Modern architects dreamed of dwellings with few walls and fewer doors at the dawn of the 20th century, inspired by startling visions like Le Corbusier's Domino House, a conceptual design for a structure with no interior walls. Walls have their purpose, nonetheless, and continue to play a key role in giving meaning to space as the 21st century begins. An attractive example of an residence where walls make their understated but indispensable appearance is a 2,000-square-foot Parisian residence designed by Jean-Pierre Heim within a typical circa 1930 apartment building clad in stone. Following a total gutting of the existing interior, Heim has introduced a suave, classical interior with a contemporary spatial orientation. So while the proper elements of the Ionic order are in place, including columns, moldings, and paneling, rooms flow into one another to let light and air penetrate everywhere. Traditional materials such as Venetian plaster on the walls, black and white marble, wood and carpet on the floor, and architectural woodworking blend convincingly with contemporary and transitional furnishings, light and colorful textiles, polished metal, mirrors and lighting fixtures. As for the walls, Heim uses them to define rooms without isolating them, so the living room and dining room are no longer cut off from each other as they were in the previous scheme. Perhaps the world is not ready for Le Corbusier's daring. On the other hand, the apartment designed by Jean-Pierre Heim demonstrates that the past can coexist in beautiful harmony with the present.

Left: A circular room highlighted by drapery and torcheres.
Right: Traditional paneling complements a contemporary bar.
Overleaf: Unobstructed views of the rooms showcase their contemporary and transitional furnishings.

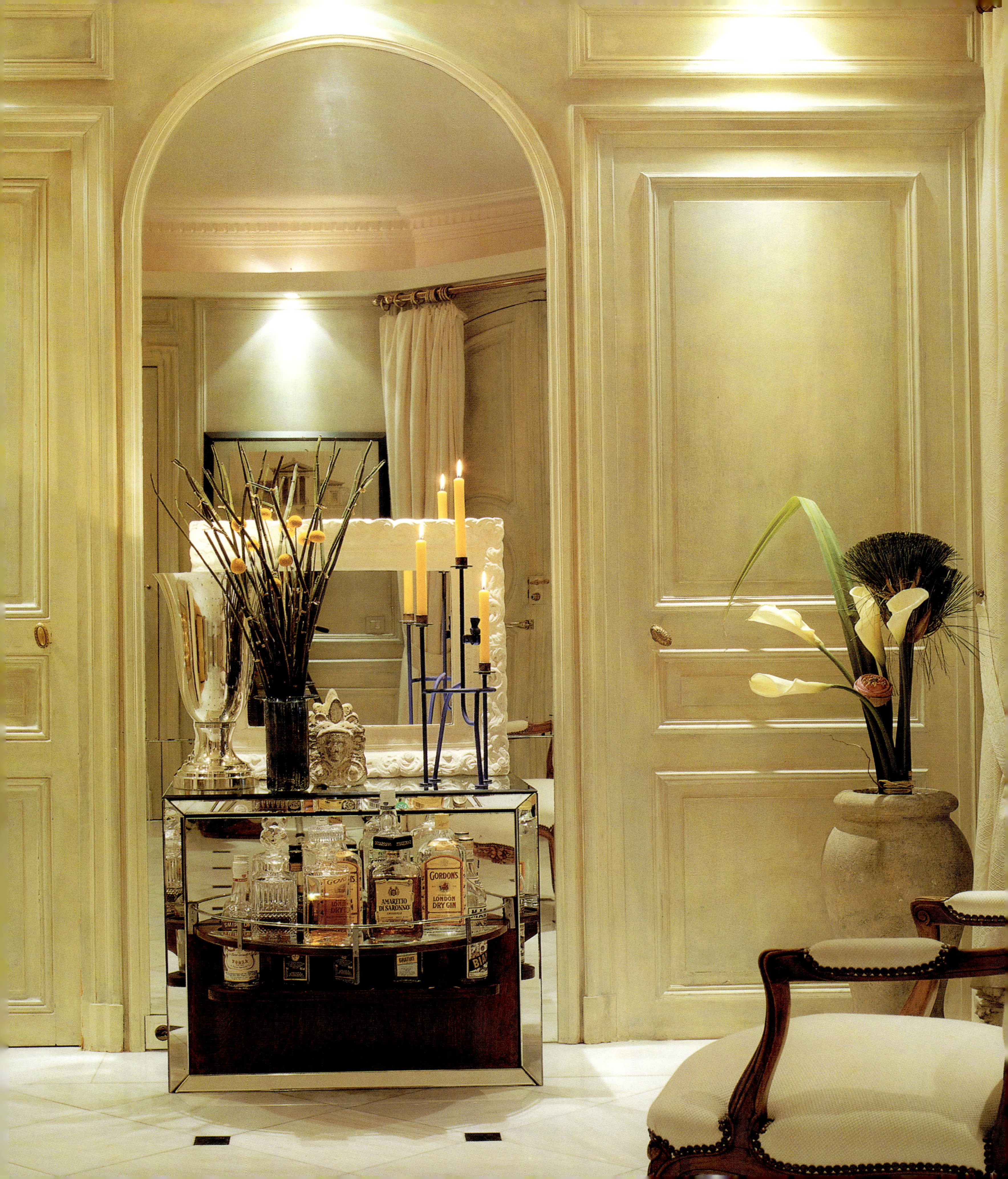
AMARETTO DI SARONNO
GORDON'S
LONDON DRY GIN

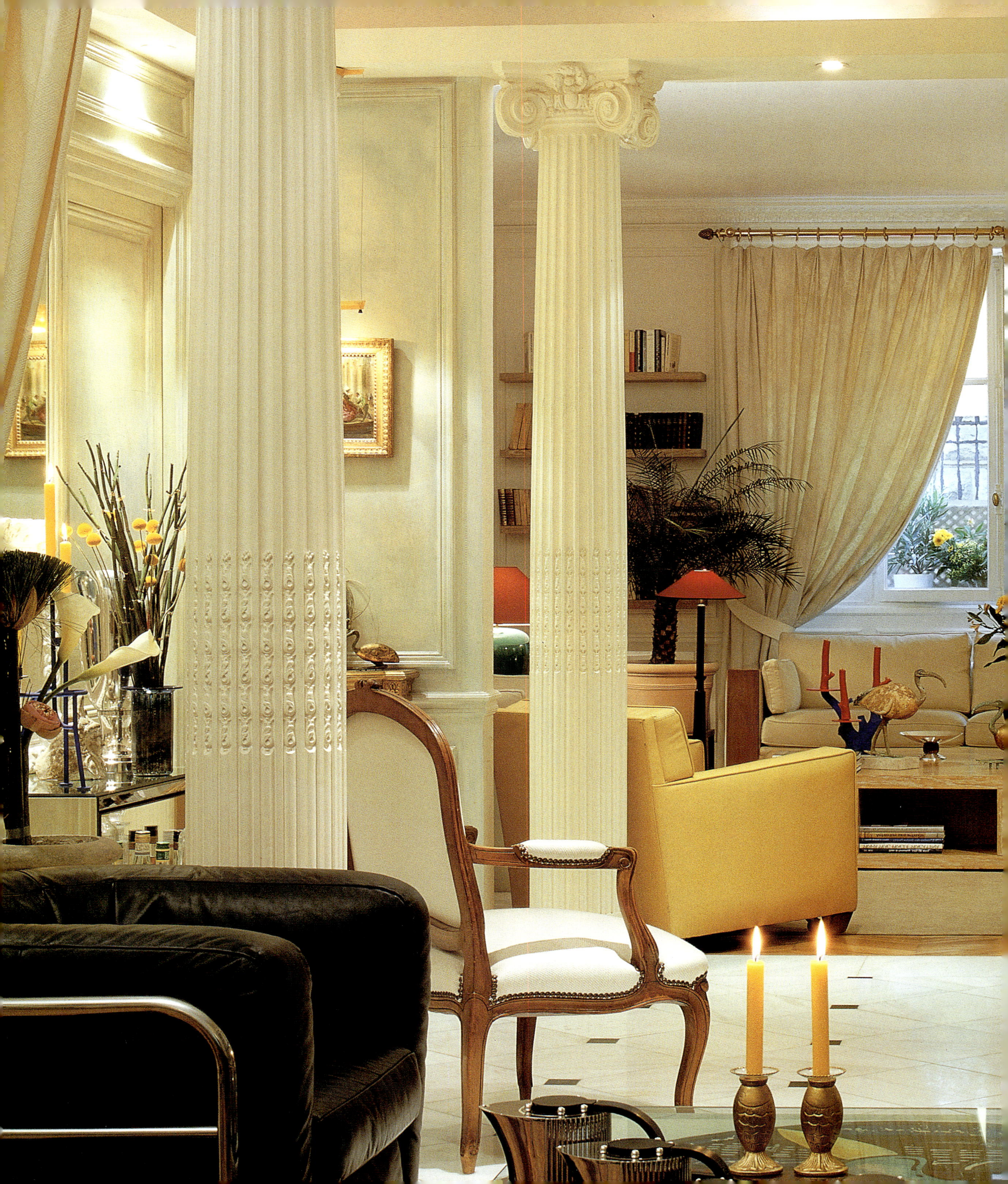

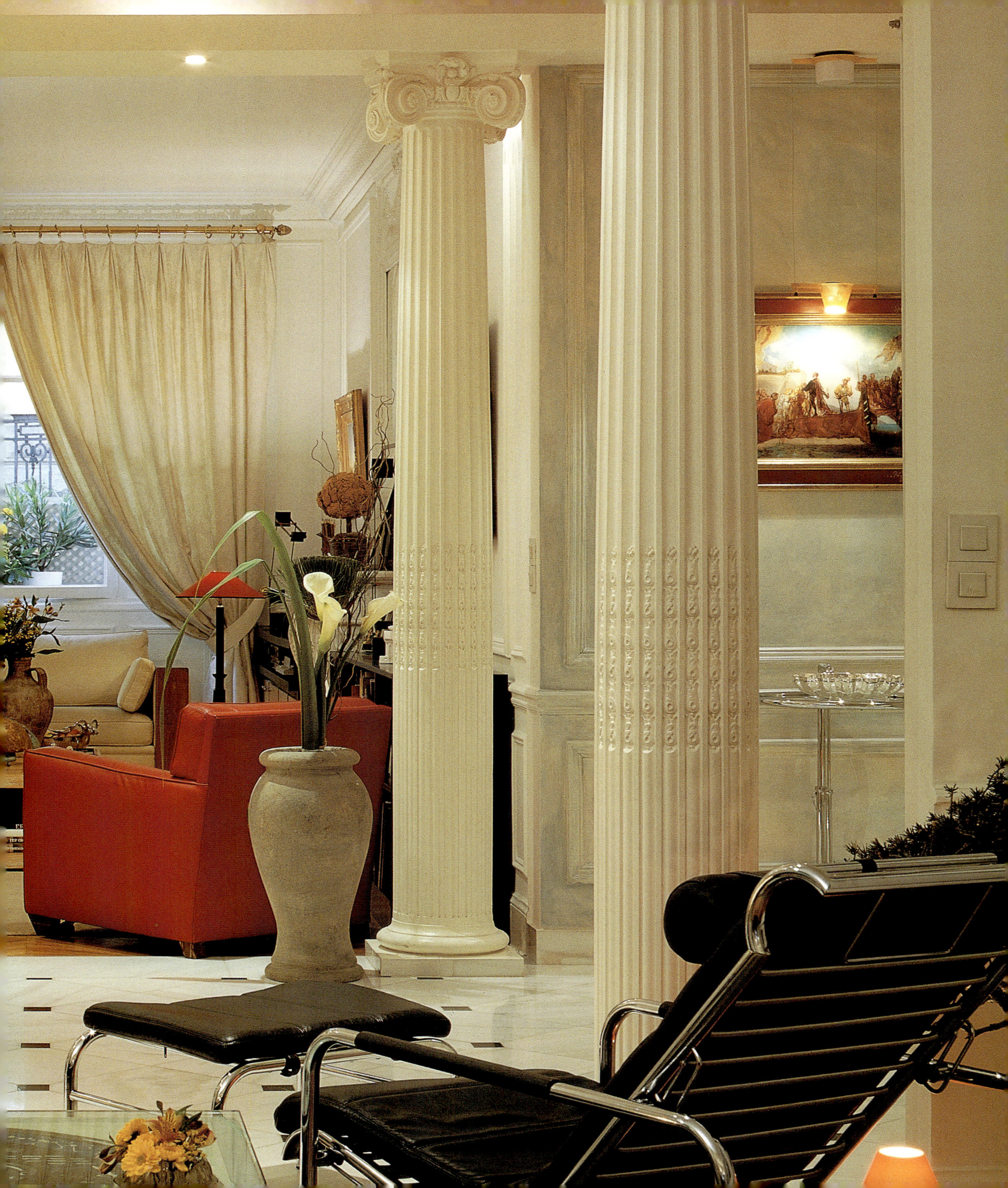

Apartment — Alwyn Court
New York, New York USA

Living space in New York, as New Yorkers will invariably complain, is almost always too tight and too dark. For Jean-Pierre Heim's renovation of a residence in Alwyn Court, a magnificent, terra-cotta-clad, French Renaissance-style apartment building designed in 1909 by the architecture firm of Harde & Short, the problem was less predictable. The apartment in this historic landmark was spacious, featuring a 650-square-foot living room, large by New York standards, and 11-foot-high ceilings, and its windows brought in light and views. However, the existing space remained dark, dingy and uninviting. To add brightness and closet space without losing the original architecture, Heim made certain critical changes. For example, walls lacking exposure to light were painted in light, clear colors, while those having exposure were painted darker, and cove lighting was added to the moldings. Because existing rooms ran directly into one another without corridors, the floor plan required careful modification to yield needed closet space. In the most noticeable alternation, Heim installed a marble checkerboard floor, Venetian stucco walls, cove lighting and a chandelier and matching sconce to dramatize the entry, a transformation Alwyn Court's flamboyant designers would surely have applauded.

This page: The remodeled living room.
Opposite: New drama for the old entry.

Trump Residence

New York, New York USA

For all his extravagant casinos, prominent New York real estate developer Donald J. Trump restrains his office buildings, downtown hotels and apartment buildings, relying on fresh interpretations of the International Style, executed in quality materials with first-rate workmanship, to project his distinctive image of luxury. His strategy is certainly evident at Trump Tower, a mixed-use, high-rise building on Manhattan's famed Fifth Avenue, designed by Der Scutt with Swanke Hayden Connell in 1983. Jean-Pierre Heim subtly acknowledges Trump Tower in his design of a jewel-like, Minimalist, two-bedroom residence on the 40th floor, where he adroitly combines existing traditional millwork with contemporary furnishings that include various icons of Modernism. The clean, sophisticated setting makes an ideal pièd á terre and home office for an owner who travels frequently on business. Since the apartment may be active at all hours, it can capture sun and views from its floor-to-ceiling windows or black out everything with screens. Heim shrewdly uses furnishings that are relatively transparent so the city becomes the apartment's principal design object, framed by yellow Venetian stucco bedroom walls, bleached wood floors, sisal rugs and the millwork. Yet the furnishings add immeasurably to the dynamics of the environment. After all, Heim has assembled the work of legendary designers like Le Corbusier and Eileen Gray and renowned manufacturers like Artemide and Flos in one compact yet memorable Manhattan apartment.

Left: Bedroom in yellow Venetian stucco.
Upper right: Black and white seating flank a Marilyn Monroe lithograph.
Lower right: One of many sweeping views of New York.
Opposite: Picture windows anchored by furniture by Le Corbusier, Eileen Gray and Philippe Starck.

The Arlington
Queens, New York USA

Left: A view of the canopy facing the street.
Far left: The canopy's new, stylized A-shaped fascia.
Lower left: Lobby interior with cherry wood paneling, new furniture and cove-lighted, curving soffit.
Opposite: The exterior passage to the front door.

Not long ago, residents entering and leaving the Arlington, a 200-unit, brick-clad apartment house in Queens, New York, took little notice of what sheltered them. Now, everyone's looking. A renovation of the canopy, landscape and lobby by Jean-Pierre Heim with architect of record Sol Niego has produced a stylish and spirited interpretation of the 1950s, when the Arlington and much of its neighborhood were built. The design achieves its unique character by reinterpreting the American design motifs of the Eisenhower years. For example, the long, narrow existing canopy was changed with the addition of a new, undulating roof that recalls the era's "organic" forms, along with cylindrical columns and a stylized, A-shaped fascia that serves as the Arlington's logo. The landscape boasts a new garden lining the exterior passage to the street, and indoor cactuses in planters. Replacing the faded lobby, Heim has installed a contemporary space with a cove-lighted, curving soffit, cherry wood paneling and reception desk, granite floor, black marble window surrounds and modern lounge seating in red and brown leather. Suddenly, turning 50 or more looks pretty enticing in Queens.

Mykonos

Mykonos, Greece

Economy and poetry invest Cycladic architecture with an unmistakable power that comes from knowing what climate and geography demand of man. Yet the outcome has been anything but prosaic, as can be seen in such traditional details as the location of stairs, size of windows, color and height. Better yet, it is a way of building that is honored today in a striking new villa on Mykonos comprising two symmetrical houses overlooking historic Delos and the Cycladic Islands. The architecture and design by Jean-Pierre Heim balances the best qualities of past and present with the ancient Cycladic builders' respect for the constraints of nature, creating a unique environment of sparkling white walls, charming bedrooms with their own baths and terraces, picturesque patios and plantings that surround the house and reflect the direction of the wind, welcoming tents and pergolas that protect terraces from the summer sun, and angled roofs that collect winter rain for later use. While the house is occupied mostly in the summer, its vernacular

Upper: A view of Delos as seen from two
Mexican chairs under a pergola.
Lower: Olive trees flourish on a
landscaped terrace outside a bedroom.
Opposite: The entrance to the patio's tents,
framed by curtains installed for wind and privacy.

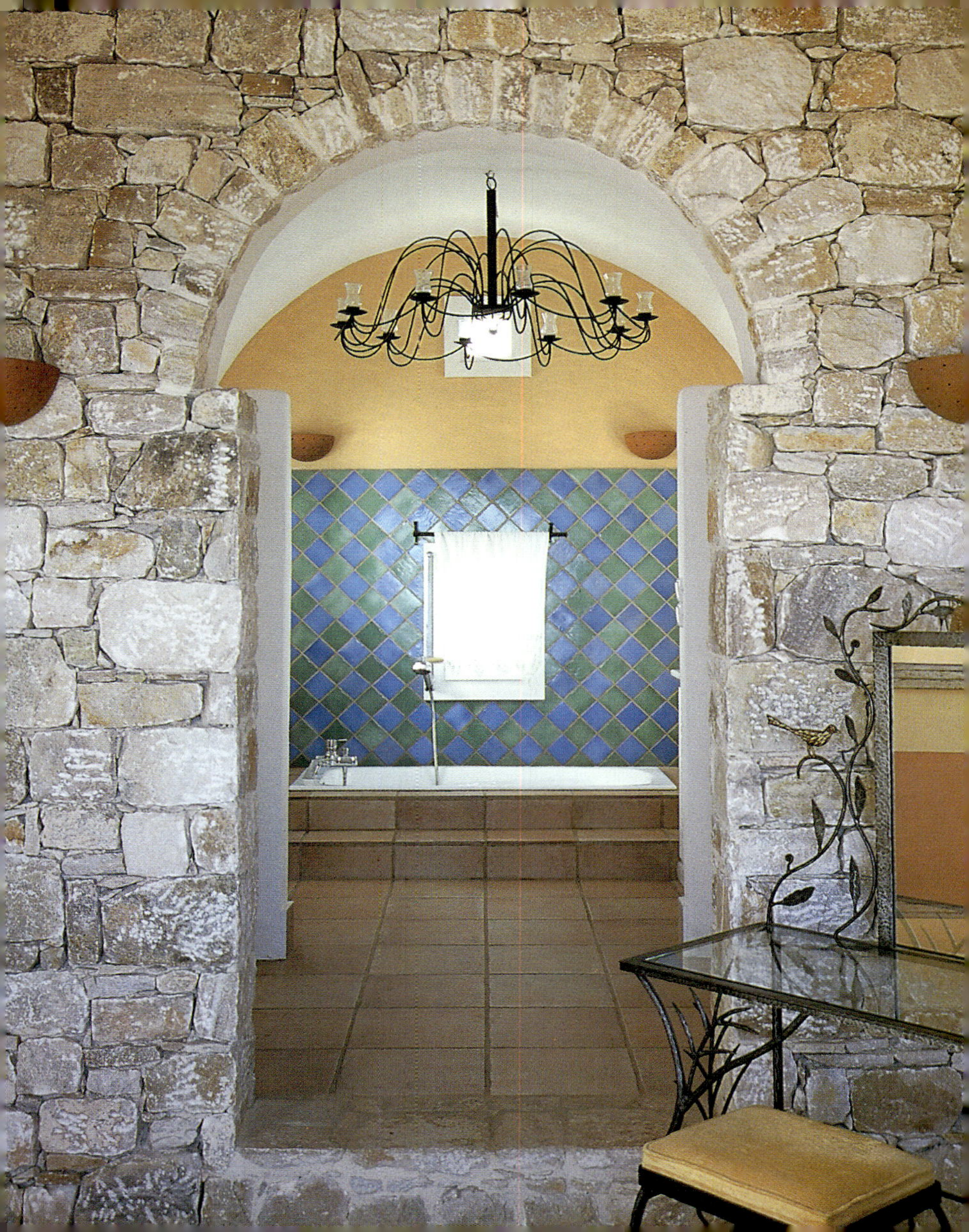

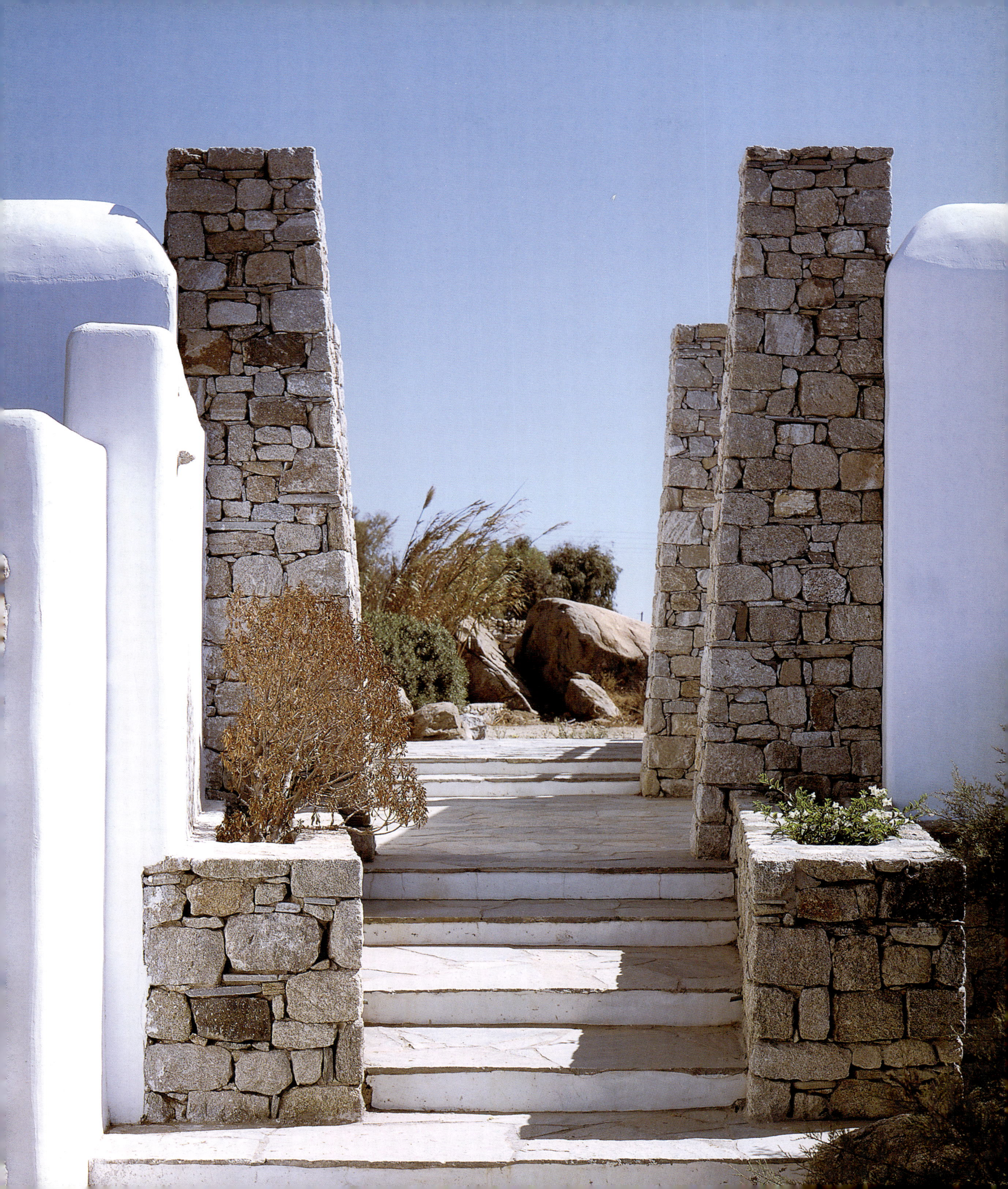

form, which complies with strict local construction laws, makes living in Mykonos a tantalizing, year-round possibility. The hardware, furnishings, and accessories have been selected with nothing less in mind, drawn from the best sources available worldwide. The outdoor living room furniture, for example, comes from Mexico, indoor furniture is the collective work of the many places where Heim has traveled, carpets, lamps and millwork are products of Morocco, iron work has been fabricated in Tunisia, and the doors represent the handicrafts of India and Saudi

Upper: The lap pool as shown in an overall view.
Lower: A close up of the pool's "salon."
Opposite: The lap as seen from inside.

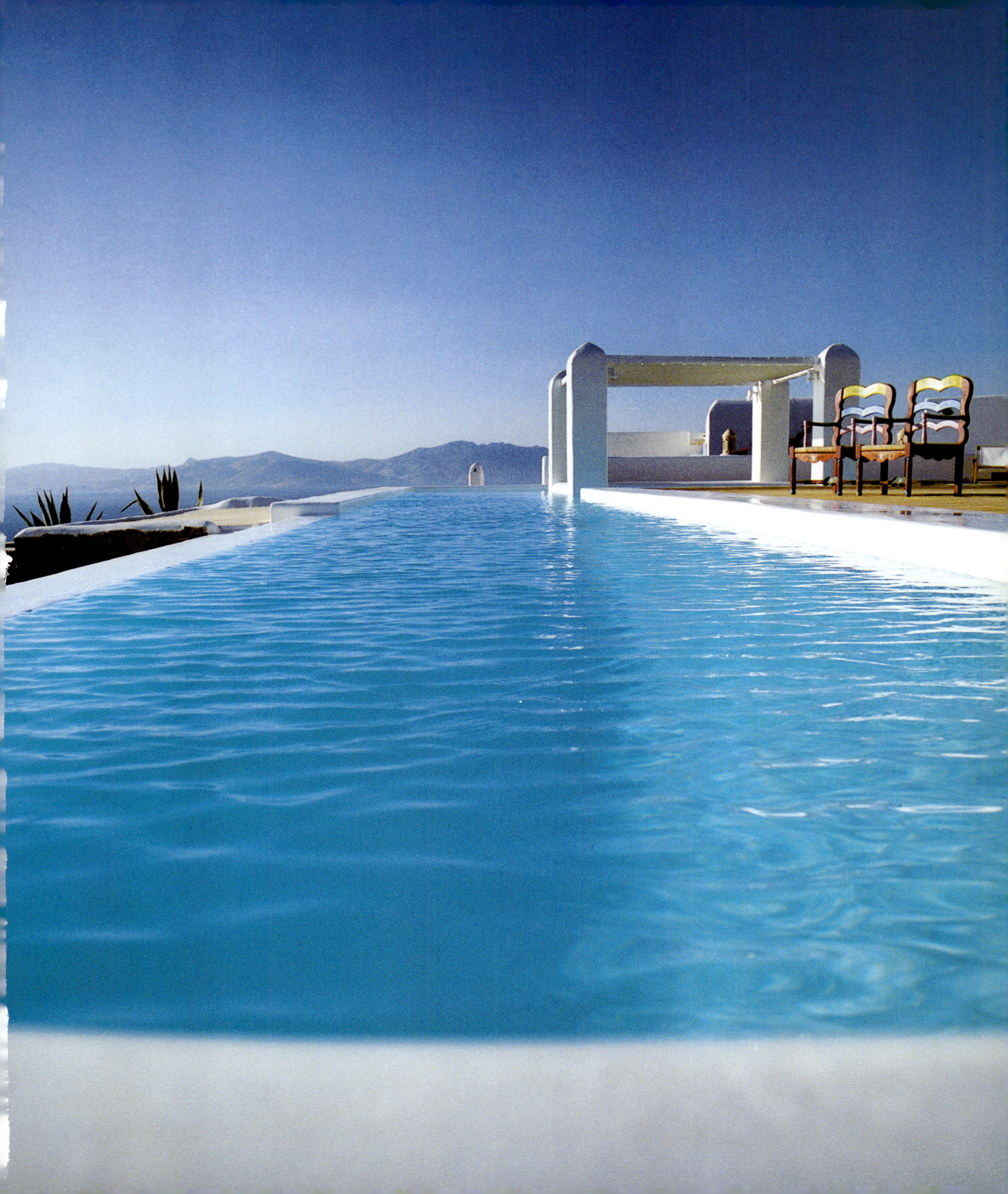

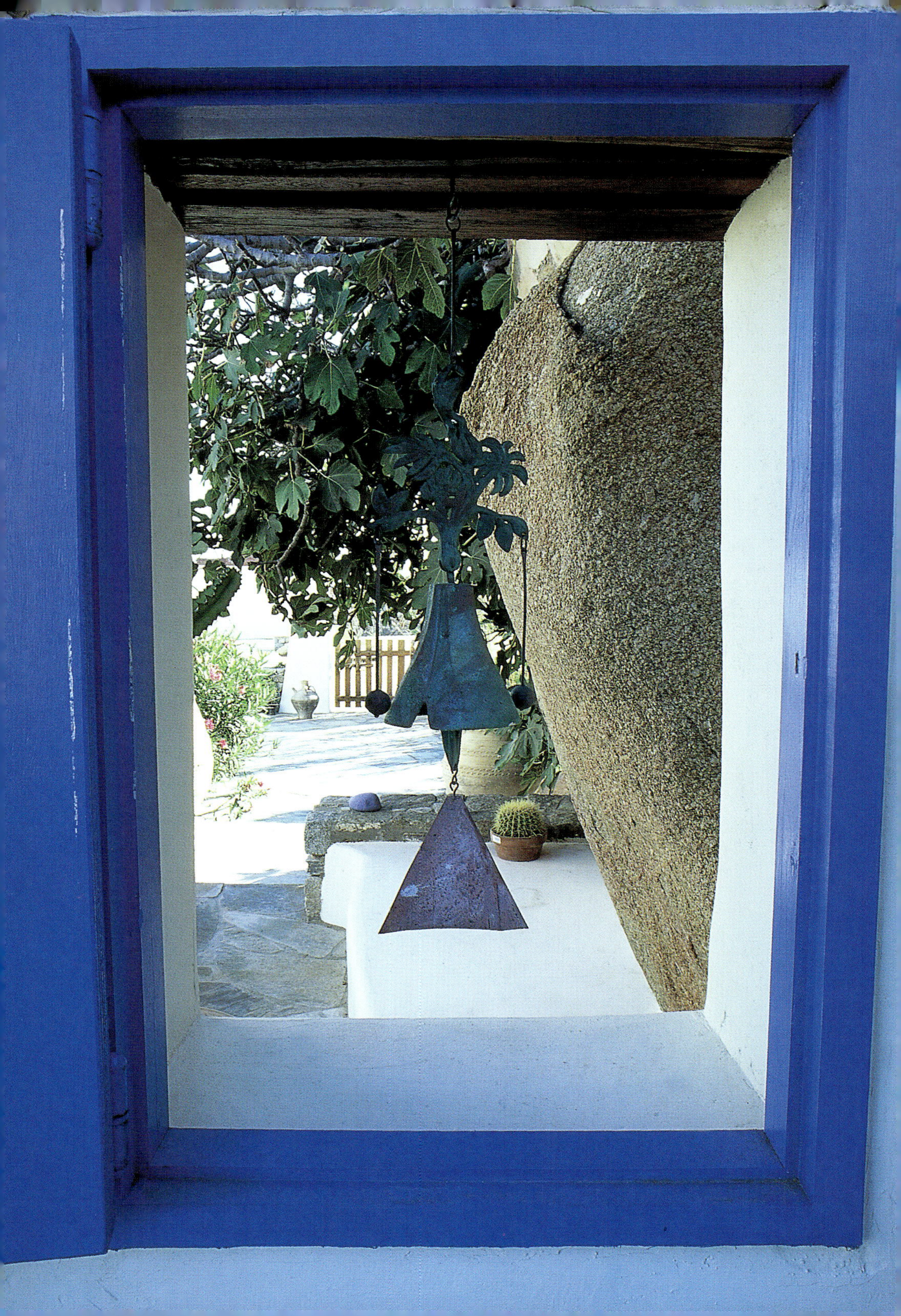

Upper: Looking to the main entrance and the Blue Rock.
Lower: Site plan.
Opposite: A blue window frame composes a view of a handcrafted bell and gardens beyond.

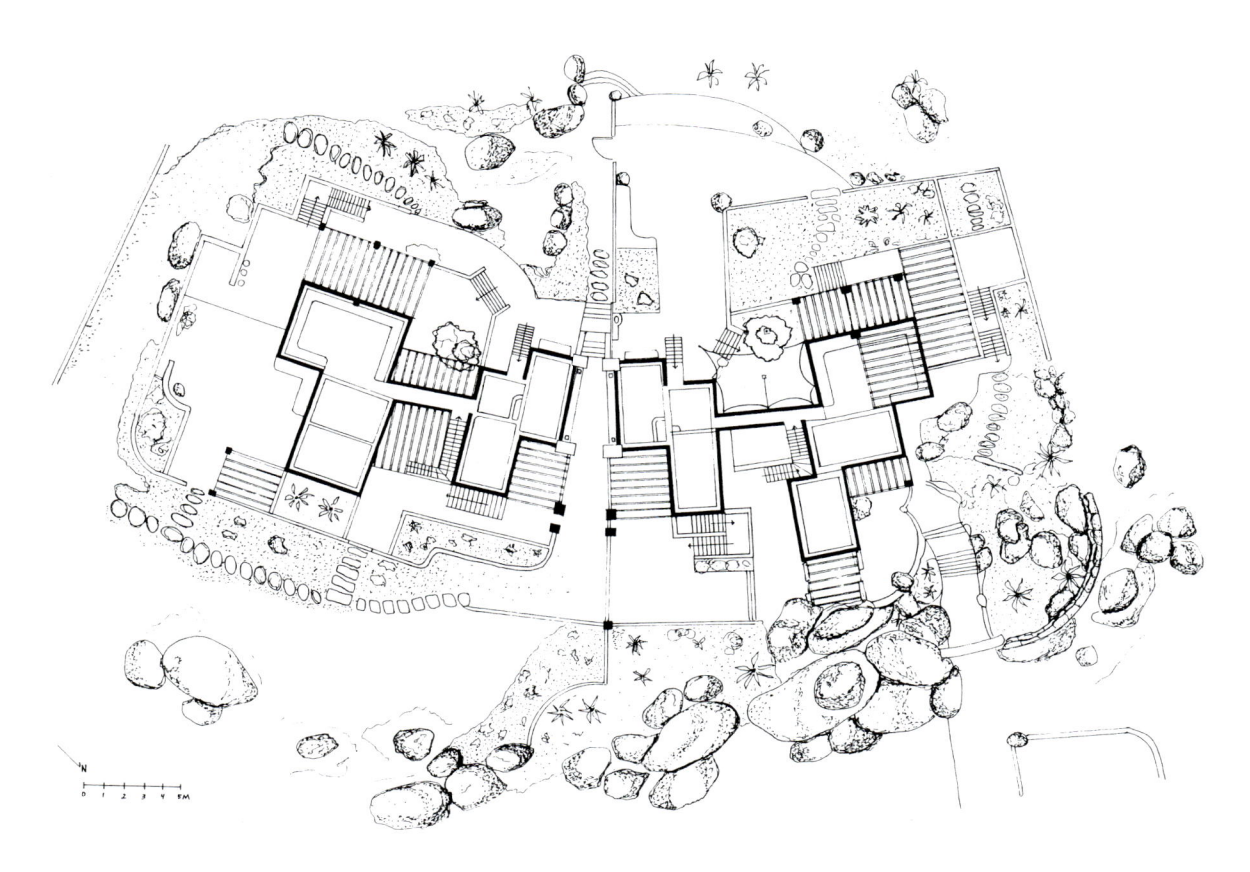

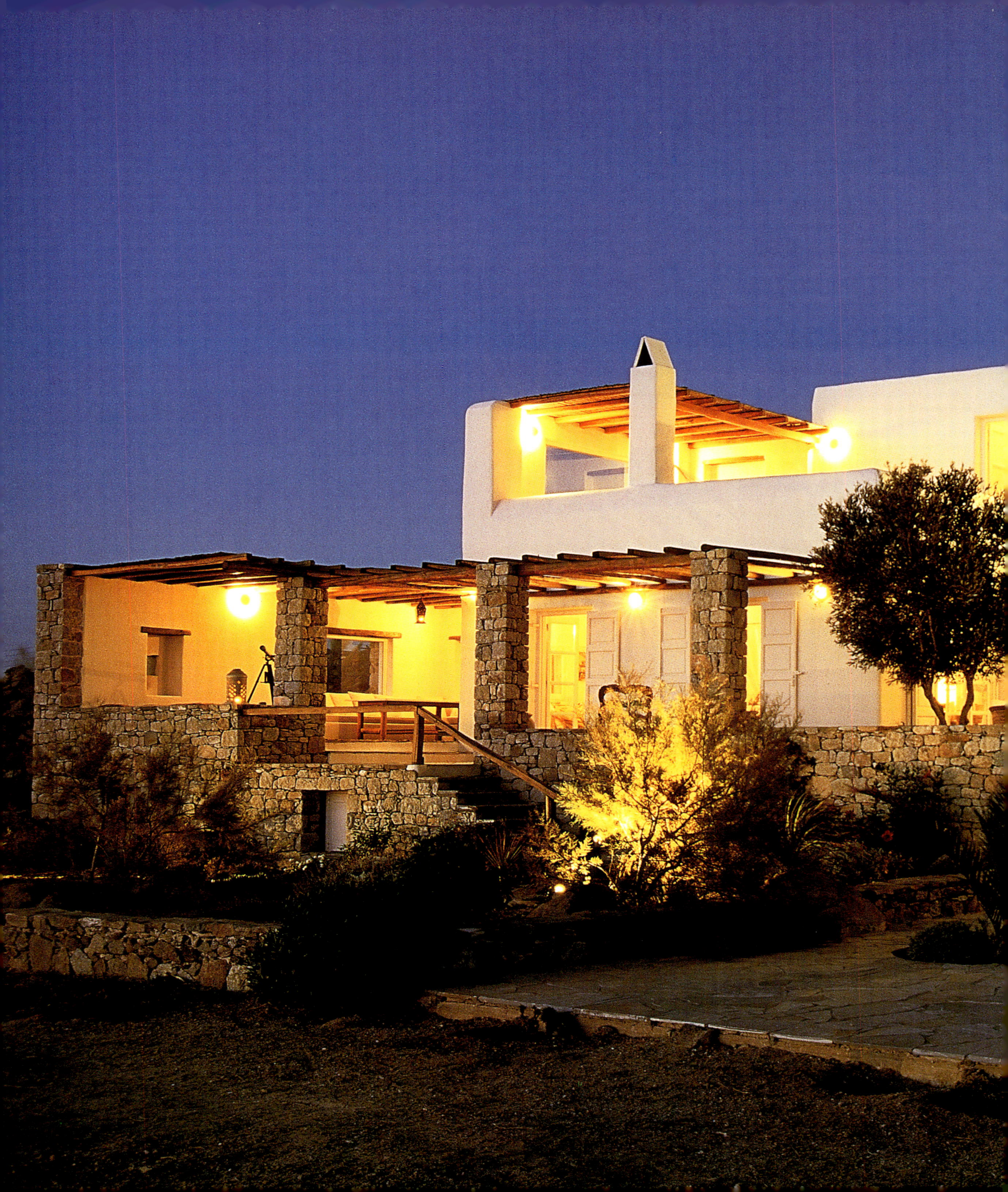

Arabia. What may best sum up the accomplishments of this project, however, is the swimming pool. A swimming pool by the sea, a man-made body of water that appears to hover at the edge of the world with an infinite horizon of 360-degre visibility surrounding the swimmer, is a profound pleasure for the eye in a dry landscape like that of Mykonos. However, creating such an idealized vision of water that would also serve as a functional piece of athletic equipment for swimming posed a considerable challenge. The land at the edge of the property's stone wall, the most desirable site for the pool, is narrow and abrupt. However, careful planning, design and construction have resulted in an alluring, canal-like, 60-foot-long, white-painted lap pool that is edged with a light-absorbing, anti-slip, colored cement surround, illuminated at night by blue halogen lighting, and symbolically interrupted by an "island" in the middle of the canal carrying a sunken dry "salon" covered with a tent. Once a swimmer is ready to leave the water, the "island" offers a quiet zone for relaxing that is like being aboard a sail boat. The joys of this man-made microcosm seem completely natural, despite the considerable effort behind its making. For Jean-Pierre Heim, the wondrous pool and the timeless house it complements symbolize what an architect can achieve by working in any of the environments — the Cycladic Islands, in this instance — he understands and appreciates.

Upper: A pergola shelters an outdoor salon.
Lower: Steps lead towards an outdoor upper terrace.
Opposite: The entrance patio offers a processional view of the house and the Cycladic Islands.
Overleaf: Rising with the sun come the views from this upper floor bedroom terrace.

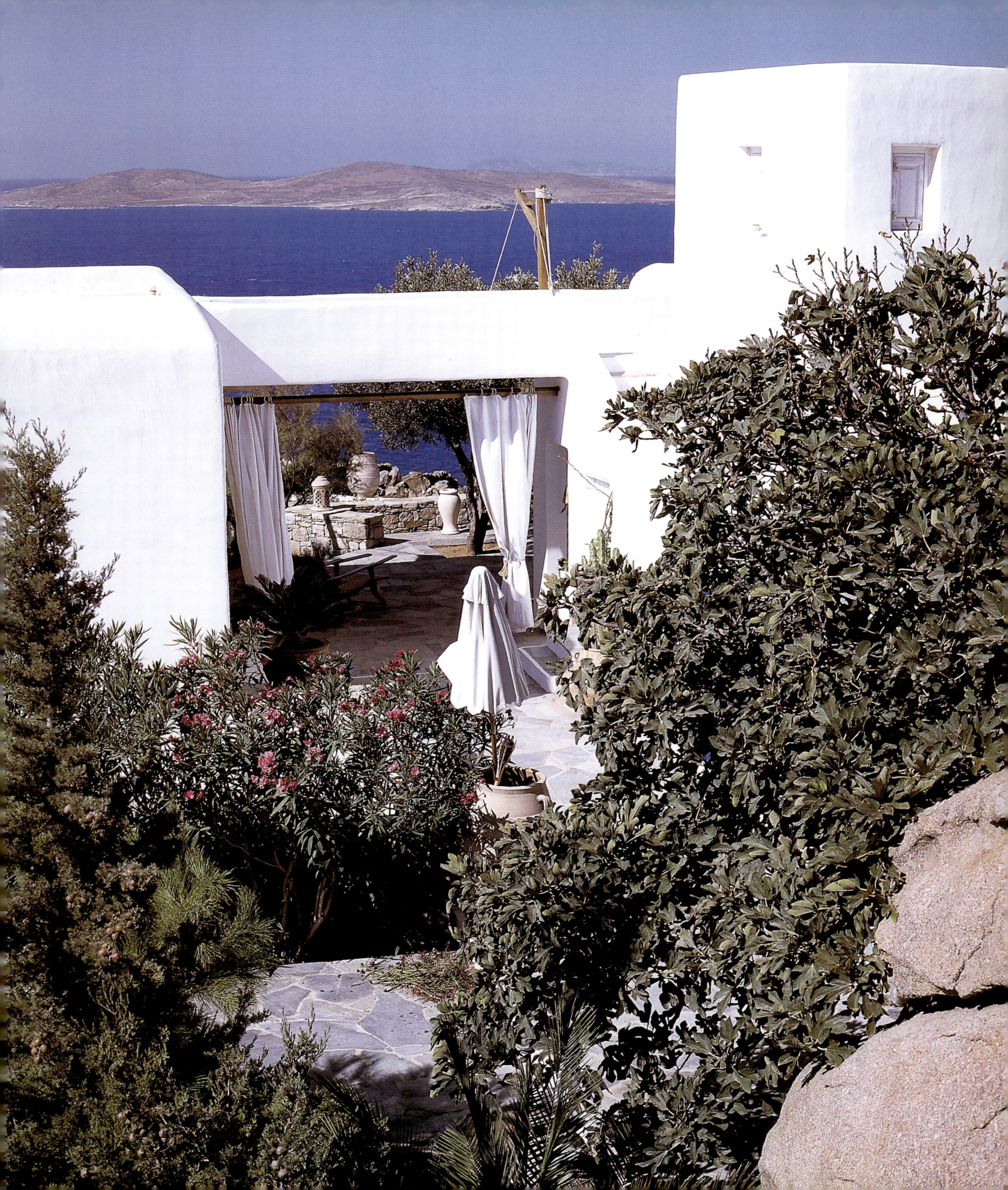

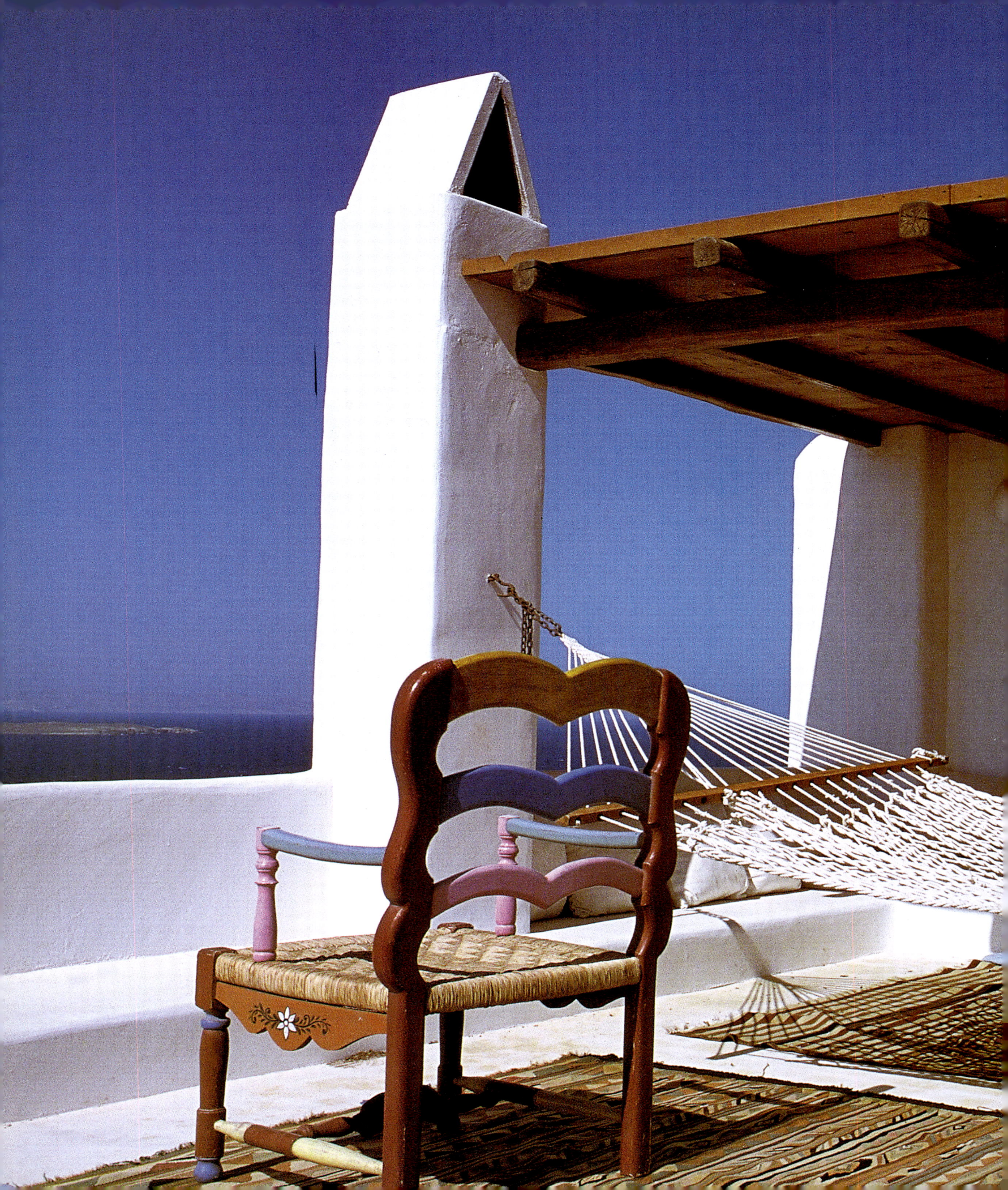

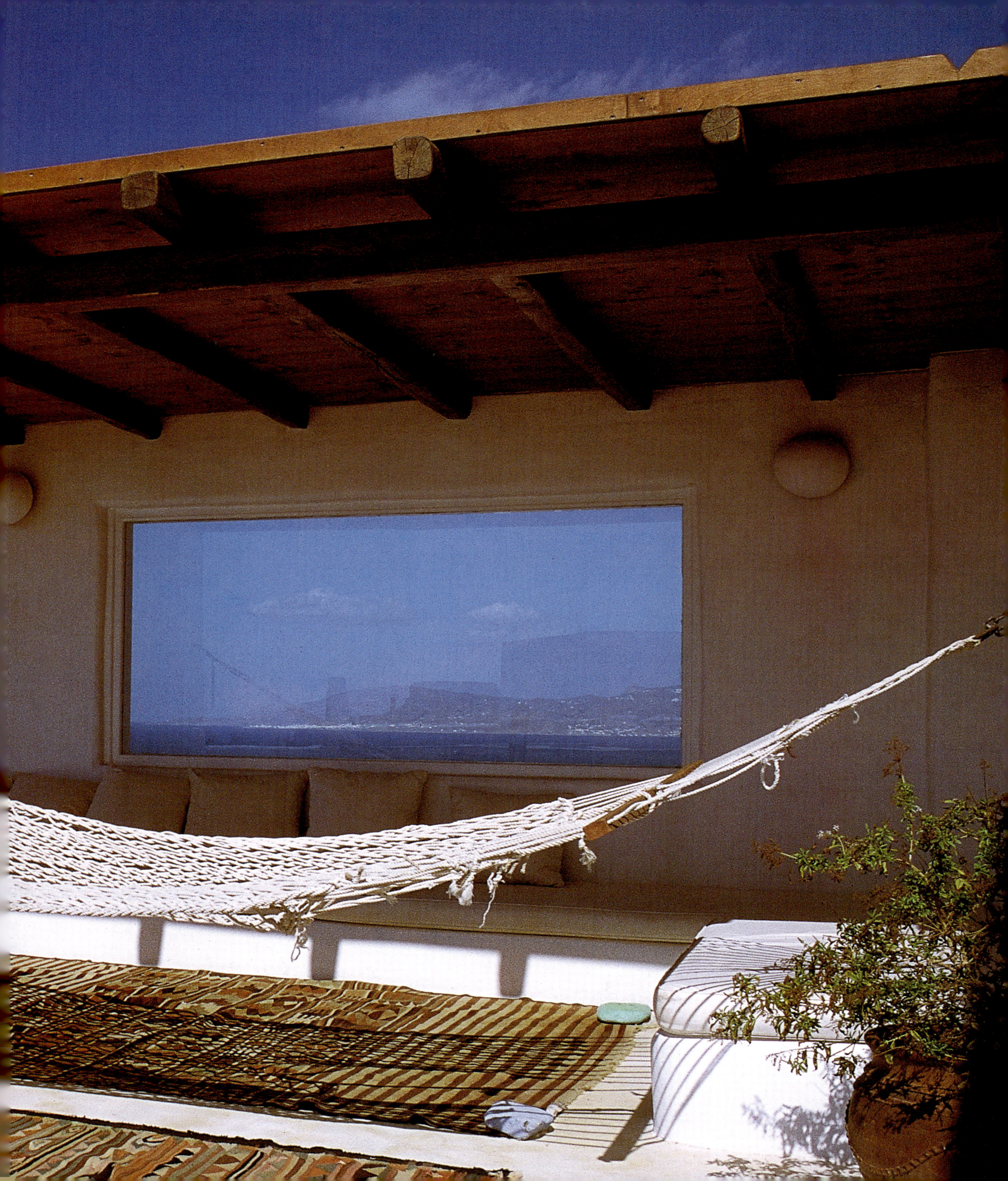

Essex House
New York, New York USA

A turning point in the recent revival of the luxury hotels and apartments at the west end of New York's Central Park South, with its romantic views of Central Park, was the restoration of Essex House, a 1930s hotel and condominium, to its former grandeur. Today, Essex House glows as an opulent showcase of Art Deco interiors that include its lobby, reception area and newly acclaimed restaurant, now supervised by famed chef Alain Ducasse. Among the elegant private residences it shelters is a new suite on the 30th floor, designed by Jean-Pierre Heim for his personal use as a residence and office. The project, which entailed a gut renovation with new kitchen and bathroom appointments, has been driven by the architect's requirements for living and working. The suite's dual nature inspired Heim to provide such facilities as the open bar kitchen facing the living room, the adjoining alcove serving as a small, private office behind a hidden pocket door, the bathroom doubling as a powder room, and the bedroom that maintains continuity within the suite using the living room's materials and colors, along with furniture specially designed for adjustability. Happily, the design's objectives go beyond meeting the functional demands of the day. Heim has chosen such materials as black granite and cherry wood in the bar kitchen, white marble and black granite in the bathroom, and oak floors and cherry wood millwork throughout the suite to acknowledge that New York is a city that dreams of art as much as it schemes about business.

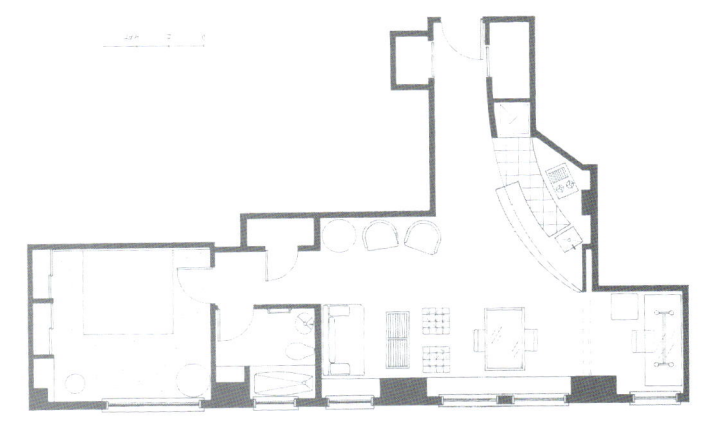

Upper: Looking from the bar kitchen to Central Park and city views
Lower: Floor plan illustrates the dual roles of the suite.
Opposite: The small, private office behind a pocket door.

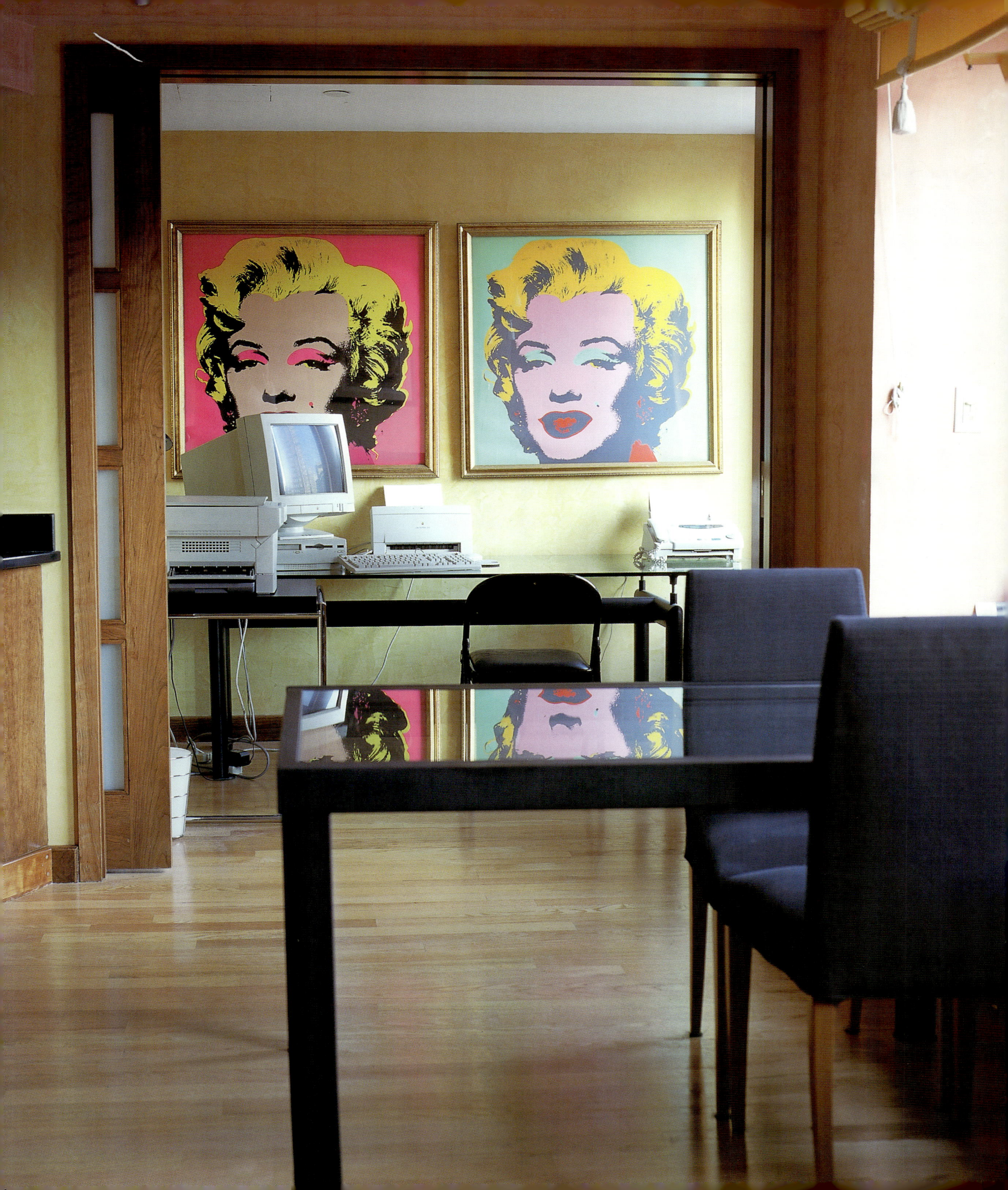

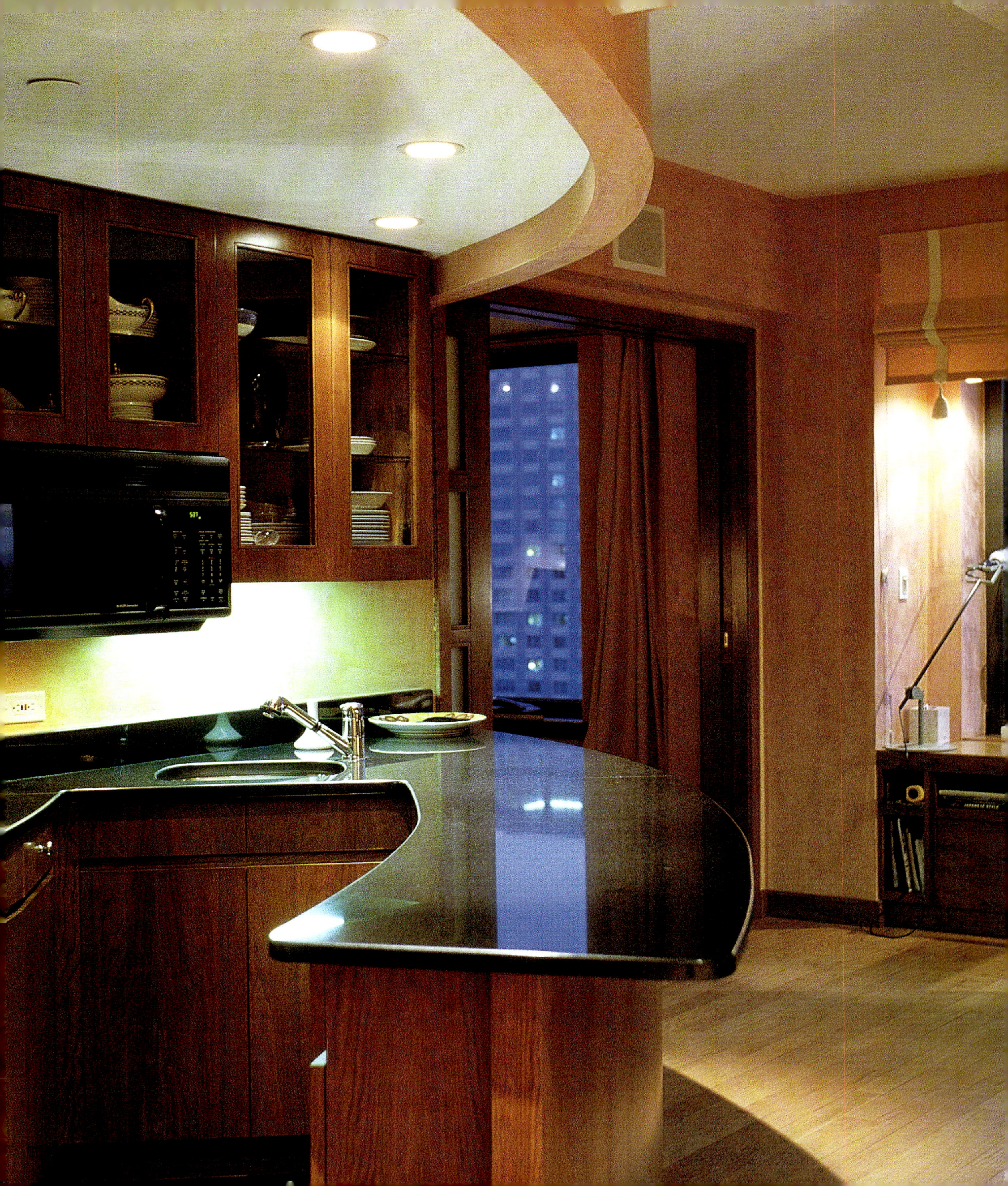

This page: Bedroom with cherry wood paneling.
Opposite: The bar kitchen and living room at twilight.

Firm Credits

AUSTRIA

1990 CHRISTIAN LACROIX BOUTIQUE DESIGN, *Salzburg*

CONGO BRAZZAVILLE

1986 PROJECT FOR THE FRENCH EMBASSY TRADE OFFICE

FRANCE

HOTELS RESTAURANTS

1989-90 PIERRE & VACANCES, LA LUNA RESTAURANT, *Cap Esterel*
1989-90 PIERRE & VACANCES, BRASSERIE DU MIDI RESTAURANT, *Cap Esterel*
1990 HOTEL LE PAVILLON, BASTILLE, *Paris*
2000 T POUR 2 CAFE RESTAURANT , *Paris*
2003 LA BRASSERIE LORRAINE, *Paris* CURRENT

OFFICE PLANNING AND BUILDINGS

1986 MAIRIE DU XVIII° OFFICES RENOVATION, *Paris*
1987 MAIRIE DU XVIII° ENTRANCE RENOVATION, *Paris*
1987-88 EDF - GDF CENTRAL HEADQUARTERS
1988-89 DMC TEXUNION OFFICES, *Paris*
1989 MAIRIE DU XVIII°, ETAT CIVIL OFFICES RENOVATION, *Paris*
1991 LANCEL OFFICES, *Paris*
1992 CAP 15 GRENELLE LOBBY AND CONFERENCE CENTER PROJECT
1996 CITAIX OFFICE BUILDING, *Chasse sur Rhone, Nangis*

PRIVATE RESIDENCES PARIS FRANCE
1979-2002

RETAIL STORES

1987 LANVIN STORE CANNES.
1987, DESCAMPS STORES PARIS: *Rue du Four*
1988-89 *Rue de Rivoli, Rue de Passy, Nation*
1987-88 DESCAMPS STORES FRANCE: *Mulhouse, Enghien, Perpignan*

1988-89 PUIFORCAT STORES PARIS: *Galeries Lafayette, Printemps Avenue Matignon, Tokyo, New York*
1990 LANCEL STORE, *Aix-en-Provence*
1990-91 LANCEL STORES, *Paris, Lyon, Lille*

1994 STEPHANE ROLLAND AVENUE, *François 1er*
1995 ICHTHYS AVENUE, *François 1er*

SAINT BARTH

2003 VILLAGE ST JEAN RENOVATION HOTEL CURRENT

GERMANY

1980 LE BISTROT 77, Restaurant, *Frankfurt*
1982 DIE LEITER, Restaurant, *Frankfurt*
1987 CHAMALEON NIGHTCLUB RESTAURANT, *Frankfurt*
1988-89 PRIVATE HOUSE, *Frankfurt*
1991 LUXOR PALACE, Nightclub, *Dresden*
1991 DIE LEITER, Restaurant, *Dresden*
1991 STADTOR ENTERTAINMENT CENTER, *Cottbuss*
1991 DIE LEITER, *Cottbuss*
1993 BABELSBERG OFFICE AND STUDIO PROJECT ENTRANCE DESIGN, *Berlin*
1995 WIESBADEN WALHALLA OPERA THEATER RESTAURANT PROJECT DESIGN
2000 CAPITOL MUSIC OPERA HOUSE, *Offenbach, Frankfurt*
2001 FRANKFURT PRIVATE HOUSE RESIDENCE

GREECE

1994 LADY CATERINA YACHT, 150 Ft. Interior and Corporate Design
1995 MYKONOS PRIVATE HOUSE DESIGN RESIDENCES.
2003 KASTORIA MACEDONIA PRIVATE HOUSE .*Current*
2003 CINEPANORAMA PROJECT PROPOSAL .*Current*

LEBANON

1995 BEIRUT S.A.D WORK EXHIBITION
1995 BEIRUT PROJECTS FOR PLAZAS

MONTE CARLO

1988 DESCAMPS STORE
1988-89 PUIFORCAT STORE

MOROCCO

1998 MARRAKECH CLUB MED PROJECT DESIGN COMPETITION
1999 TANGIERS CLUB MED YASMINA VILLAGE, Renovation 450 Rooms

SAUDI ARABIA

1988	FRENCH TRADE OFFICES DESIGN AT THE FRENCH EMBASSY, *Riad*
1988	FRENCH EMBASSY APARTMENTS RENOVATIONS, *Riad*

SENEGAL

1999	DAKAR CLUB MED LES ALMADIES RENOVATION 400 ROOMS

USA

RESTAURANTS AND HOTELS DESIGN

1979-81	PRONTO RESTAURANTS DESIGN, *Mineapolis, Baltimore, Atlanta, Houston, Washington DC*
1980	RAOUL'S TROMPE L'OEIL DESIGN RESTAURANT *SoHo*
1983	AMAZONAS, BRAZILIAN RESTAURANT, *New York*
1984	AMAZONAS PROJECT DESIGN, *Chicago*
1987-88	10:10 RESTAURANT, BULOVA CORPORATE CENTER, *La Guardia, New York*
2000	ABAJOUR, *New York*
2002	THALASSA RESTAURANT TRIBECA, *New York*

MURAL PAINTINGS, INTERIOR DESIGN OF PRIVATE RESIDENCES DESIGN

1980	MURAL PAINTING FOR A PRIVATE RESIDENCE, *Long Island*
1980	TROMPE L'OEIL AND APARTMENT DESIGN *Thompson Street, New York*
1984	APARTMENT, CARLYLE HOTEL, *New York*
1984	HOUSE TROMPE L'OEIL, QUOQUE *Long Island*
1994	MIAMI RESIDENCE PALM ISLAND, *Miami, Florida*
1998	APARTMENT, Alwyn Court, 7th Avenue, *New York*
1998	APARTMENT, Essex House, *New YorK*
2000	APARTMENT, Olympic Tower, Fifth Avenue, *New York*
2001	APARTMENT, Trump Tower, Fifth Avenue, *New York*
2001	APARTMENT, Upper West Side, *New York*
2001	APARTMENT, Tribeca Loft, New York
2001	APARTMENT, Upper East Side, New York

STORES

1985	LA CHAUSSERIA DESIGN, *New York*
1985	CATHERINE ATZEN DESIGN, Logo, Packaging, Interior Design, Beauty Salon, *New York*
1986-88	LANVIN STORE & OFFICES, MADISON AVENUE, *New York*
1987	DESCAMPS, Columbus Avenue, *New York*
1988	LOTHAR STORE, *New York*
1988	PUIFORCAT STORE, Madison Avenue, *New York*
1989	DESCAMPS MADISON AVENUE, Columbus Avenue, Madison Avenue, *New York*
1994	LE CORDON BLEU, NEW YORK TRUMP PLAZA
1995	CATIMINI DESIGN, *New York*
1995	BACCARAT, Madison Avenue, *New York*
1996	REVILLON, Fifth Avenue, *New York*
1998	VAN CLEEF AND ARPELS, Façade, Fifth Avenue, *New York*
2002	MAUD FRIZON STORE, Lexington Avenue, *New York*

OFFICE SHOWROOM PLANNING DESIGN AND BUILDING LOBBY DESIGN

1987	FRENCH TRADE OFFICE, FRENCH EMBASSY OFFICES, *New York*
1982	HIGH TIMES OFFICES, DESIGN ENTRANCE *New York*
1988	FRENCH GOVERNMENT TOURIST OFFICE, 5th Avenue, *New York*
1989	BRITISH AIRWAYS LOBBY, Bulova building *New York*
1990	MCA. RECORDS, PRESIDENT'S OFFICE DESIGN, *New York*
1991	MCA LOBBY DESIGN
1989	ALES GROUP SHOWROOM AND OFFICES, *New York*
1994	2 EAST END AVENUE HALLWAY RENOVATION, *New York*
1994	CDC BANK TRADE OFFICE DESIGN CAISSE DES DEPOTS TRADE OFFICE, Bank Renovation
1997	GAZELLE COSMETIC SHOWROOM, 507 Madison Avenue, *New York*
1999	THE ARLINGTON LOBBY RENOVATION, *Kew Gardens, Queens*
2001	EAST 85 STREET HALLWAY RENOVATION, *New York*
2002	PROPOSAL GROUND ZERO DEVELOPMENT WORLD TRADE CENTER, *New York*

Credits

Photography credit

Thalassa, Abajour, Bulova 30, Lobby , Bulova lobby 32/33 Trump residence, The Arlington, Essex House : Costas Picadas

Capitol Music Theater :Capitol , Jean-Pierre Heim.

Bulova 26, 28, 29, French trade office Embassy, Christian Lacroix, : Serge Hambourg.

Club Med, Luxor Palace, Chameleon, Hotel Pavillon Bastille, Ichthys, Puiforcat, Nicolas Feuillatte, Lancel, Assomption Church, Paris City Hall, Citaix, Apartment 1 Paris, Apartment 2 Paris,: Fabrice Rambert.

Yasmina hotel: Jean-Pierre Heim

Revillon, Baccarat, Apartment Alwyn court : Philippe Houze

Die Leiter: Francis Rambert

Trompe l'oeil : Francis Rambert 130/131-134 , Jean-Pierre Heim 135, P.Heying 132/133-

Egyptian line: J-E Fortunier

Furniture line: P. Heying

Mykonos house: Milan Josipovic.
Photo :Jean-Pierre Heim : Milan Josipovic and back of cover

Cover Photo : Costas Picadas

INDIVIDUALS : who participated to those projects .

Credits to :

Christine Heim.
Tyrone Roper .
Remy de Bourbon –Parme.
Galal Mahmoud.
Ibrahim Chaoul.
Armando Milani.
Guillaume Saalburg.
Suzan Blumenfeld.
The Philips group.
Sol Niego
Pascal Langevin
Daniel Brandt.
Mattia Montanile.
Bernard Joly.
Kevin Stone .
Marijana Sarich.
Michelle Ballard
Andreas Vasillaros